Helping Students Understand Algebra II

By

BARBARA SANDALL, Ed.D., and MELFRIED OLSON, Ed.D.

COPYRIGHT © 2005 Mark Twain Media, Inc.

ISBN   10-digit: 1-58037-301-1
          13-digit: 978-1-58037-301-2

Printing No. CD-404028

Mark Twain Media, Inc., Publishers
Distributed by Carson-Dellosa Publishing Company, Inc.

HPS 221344

Table of Contents

Introduction

The *Helping Students Understand Math series* will introduce students in middle school and high school to the topics of Pre-Algebra, Algebra, and Algebra II. Geometry will also be included in this series. All of the worktexts will be aligned with the National Council of Teachers of Mathematics (NCTM) *Principles and Standards for School Mathematics.*

This series is written for classroom teachers, parents, families, and students. The worktexts in this series can be used as a full unit of study or as individual lessons to supplement textbooks or curriculum programs. Parents and students can use this series as an enhancement to what is being done in the classroom or as a tutorial at home. All students will benefit from these activities, but the series was designed with the struggling math student in mind. The **concepts** and **explanations** for the concepts are described in simple **step-by-step instructions** with **examples** in the introduction of each lesson. Students will be given practice problems using the concepts introduced and descriptions of real-life applications of the concepts.

According to the Mathematics Education Trust and NCTM, new technologies require the fundamentals of algebra, and algebraic thinking should be a part of the background for all citizens. These technologies also provide opportunities to generate numerical examples, graph data, analyze patterns, and make generalizations. An understanding of algebra is also important because business and industry require higher levels of thinking and problem solving.

NCTM Standards suggest content and vocabulary are necessary but of equal importance are the processes of mathematics. The process skills described in the *Standards* include problem solving, reasoning, communication, and connections. The worktexts in this series will address both the content and processes of algebra and algebraic thinking. This worktext, *Helping Students Understand Algebra II,* will help students transition from Algebra to Algebra II.

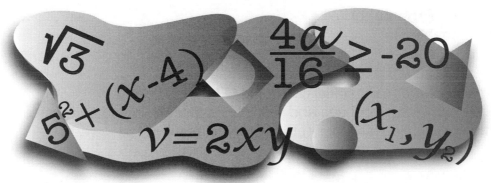

Teacher Note: For the purposes of this subject, it is not necessary for students to convert improper fractions to mixed numbers.

Principles and Standards for School Mathematics (NCTM)

Number and Operations
Students will be enabled to:
- ☐ Understand numbers, ways of representing numbers, relationships among numbers, and number systems.
- ☐ Understand meanings of operations and how they relate to one another.
- ☐ Compute fluently and make reasonable estimates.

Algebra
Students will be enabled to:
- ☐ Understand patterns, relations, and functions.
- ☐ Represent and analyze mathematical situations and structures using algebraic symbols.
- ☐ Use mathematical models to represent and understand quantitative relationships.
- ☐ Analyze change in various contexts.

Geometry
Students will be enabled to:
- ☐ Analyze characteristics and properties of two- and three-dimensional geometric shapes and develop mathematical arguments about geometric relationships.
- ☐ Specify locations and describe spatial relationships using coordinate geometry and other representational systems.
- ☐ Apply transformations and use symmetry to analyze mathematical situations.
- ☐ Use visualization, spatial reasoning, and geometric modeling to solve problems.

Measurement
Students will be enabled to:
- ☐ Understand measurable attributes of objects and the units, systems, and processes of measurement.
- ☐ Apply appropriate techniques, tools, and formulas to determine measurements.

Data Analysis and Probability
Students will be enabled to:
- ☐ Formulate questions that can be addressed with data and collect, organize, and display relevant data to answer them.
- ☐ Select and use appropriate statistical methods to analyze data.
- ☐ Develop and evaluate inferences and predictions that are based on data.
- ☐ Understand and apply basic concepts of probability.

NCTM Standards and Expectations Grades 9–12 Algebra (NCTM)

Algebra Instructional programs from grade 9 through grade 12 should enable all students to:

Understand patterns, relations, and functions

- Generalize patterns using explicitly defined and recursively defined functions.
- Understand relations and functions and select, convert flexibly among, and use various representations of them.
- Analyze functions of one variable by investigating rates of change, intercepts, zeros, asymptotes, and local and global behavior.
- Understand and perform transformations such as arithmetically combining, composing, and inverting commonly used fractions, using technology to perform such operations on more complicated symbolic expressions.
- Understand and compare the properties of classes of functions, including exponential, polynomial, rational, logarithmic, and periodic functions.
- Interpret representations of functions of two variables.

Represent and analyze mathematical situations and structures using algebraic symbols

- Understand the meaning of equivalent forms of expressions, equations, inequalities, and relations.
- Write equivalent forms of equations, inequalities, and systems of equations and solve them with fluency—mentally or with paper and pencil in simple cases and using technology in all cases.
- Use symbolic algebra to represent and explain mathematical relationships;
- Use a variety of symbolic representations, including recursive and parametric equations, for functions and relations.
- Judge the meaning, utility, and reasonableness of the results of symbol manipulations, including those carried out by technology.

Use mathematical models to represent and understand quantitative relationships

- Identify essential quantitative relationships in a situation and determine the class or classes of functions that might model the relationships.
- Use symbolic expressions, including interactive and recursive forms, to represent relationships arising from various contexts.

Analyze change in various contexts

- Approximate and interpret rates of change from graphical and numerical data.

Common Mathematics Symbols and Terms

Term	Symbol/Definition	Example
Addition sign	+	$2 + 2 = 4$
Subtraction sign	−	$4 - 2 = 2$
Multiplication sign	or a dot • or 2 numbers or letters together or parentheses	3 2 $2 • 2$ $2x$ $2(2)$
Division sign	÷ or a slash mark (/) or a horizontal fraction bar, or $\overline{}$	$6 ÷ 2$ $4/2$ $\frac{4}{2}$ $2\overline{)4}$
Equals or is equal to	=	$2 + 2 = 4$
Does Not Equal	≠	$5 ≠ 1$
Parentheses – symbol for grouping numbers	( )	$(2 \quad 5) + 3 =$
Pi – a number that is approximately 22/7 or ≈ 3.14	π	$3.1415926\ldots$
Negative number – to the left of zero on a number line	-	-3
Positive number – to the right of zero on a number line	+	+4
Less than	<	$2 < 4$
Greater than	>	$4 > 2$
Greater than or equal to	≥	$2 + 3 ≥ 4$
Less than or equal to	≤	$2 + 1 ≤ 4$
Is approximately	≈	$\pi ≈ 3.14$
Radical sign	$\sqrt{}$	$\sqrt{9}$ The square root of 9 $\sqrt[3]{27}$ The cube root of 27
The *n*th power of *a*	a^n	$3^2 = 9$

Common Mathematics Symbols and Terms (cont.)

Variables	Are letters used for unknown numbers	$x + 8 = 12$ x is the letter representing the unknown number or variable
Mathematical Sentence	Contains two mathematical phrases joined by an equals (=) or an inequality ($\neq, <, >, \leq, \geq$) sign	$2 + 3 = 5$ $9 - 3 > 5$ $3x + 8 = 20$ $4 + 2 \neq 5$
Equation	Mathematical sentence in which two phrases are connected with an equals (=) sign.	$5 + 7 = 12$ $3x = 12$ $1 = 1$
Mathematical Operations	Mathematics has four basic operations: addition, subtraction, multiplication, and division. Symbols are used for each operation.	+ sign indicates addition – sign indicates subtraction ÷ indicates division • or indicates multiplication
Like Terms	Can be all numbers or variables that are the same letter and same exponent	$3, 4, 5$ $3c, -5c, \frac{1}{2}c$; the variable is the same with the same exponent; they are like terms
Unlike Terms	Can be numbers or variables that are different	$5 + a$; cannot be added because they are unlike terms. $3x + 4y + 1z$; cannot be added because the variables are different, so they are unlike terms
Coefficient	The number in front of the variable (letter for the unknown number)	$5x$ In this number, 5 is the coefficient.
Identity Property of Addition	Any number or variable added to zero is that number or variable.	$0 + 5 = 5$ $-3 + 0 = -3$ $a + 0 = a$
Identity Property of Multiplication	Any number or variable times 1 is equal to that number or variable.	$12 • 1 = 12$ $b • 1 = b$ $3y • 1 = 3y$

Common Mathematics Symbols and Terms (cont.)

Commutative Property of Addition	No matter the order in which you add two numbers, the sum is always the same.	$4 + 7 = 7 + 4$ $b + c = c + b$
Commutative Property of Multiplication	No matter the order in which you multiply two numbers, the answer is always the same.	$20 \cdot \frac{1}{2} = \frac{1}{2} \cdot 20$ $5 \cdot 3 = 3 \cdot 5$ $a \cdot b = b \cdot a$
Associative Property of Addition	When you add three numbers together, the sum will be the same no matter how you group the numbers.	$(5 + 6) + 7 = 5 + (6 + 7)$ $(a + b) + c = a + (b + c)$
Associative Property of Multiplication	No matter how you group the numbers when you multiply, the answer will always be the same product.	$(5 \cdot 4) \cdot 8 = 5 \cdot (4 \cdot 8)$ $(a \cdot b) \cdot c = a \cdot (b \cdot c)$
Distributive Property of Multiplication Over Addition	Allows the choice of multiplication followed by addition or addition followed by multiplication.	$3(5 + 2) = 3 \cdot 5 + 3 \cdot 2$ $a(b + c) = a \cdot b + a \cdot c$
Inverse Operation	Operation that cancels another operation	Multiplication and division $5 \cdot x = 5x$ $\frac{5x}{5} = x$ Addition and Subtraction $n + 5 - 5 = n$
Reciprocal or Multiplicative Inverse Property	Two reciprocals are multiplied, and the product is 1.	For any non-zero number: $\text{Number} \cdot \frac{1}{\text{Number}} = 1$ $\frac{1}{\text{Number}} \cdot \text{Number} = 1$ $a \cdot \frac{1}{a} = 1$ $5 \cdot \frac{1}{5} = 1$

Common Mathematics Symbols and Terms (cont.)

Exponents	Shorthand for repeated multiplication	$a^2 = a \bullet a$ $y^4 = y \bullet y \bullet y \bullet y$
Square Numbers	The result of multiplying a number or variable by itself	$4 \bullet 4 = 16$ $a \bullet a = a^2$
Square Roots	A square root indicated by the radical sign $\sqrt{}$ is the number multiplied by itself to get the radicand.	$\sqrt{9}$ What number multiplied by itself = 9? $3 \bullet 3 = 9$ So $\sqrt{9} = 3$
Radicand	Number under the radical	$\sqrt{9}$ 9 is the radicand.
Index	Number inside the radical crook tells how many times the number must be multiplied by itself.	$\sqrt[3]{27}$ 3 is the index What number multiplied by itself 3 times equals the radicand (27)?
Numerator	Top number in a fraction	$\frac{3}{5}$ In this fraction, 3 is the numerator.
Denominator	Bottom number in a fraction	$\frac{3}{5}$ In this fraction, 5 is the denominator.
Integers	Natural numbers, their opposites, or negative numbers, and zero	Set of integers: $\{... -3, -2, -1, 0, 1, 2, 3 ...\}$
Additive Inverse Property of Addition	The sum of an integer and its opposite integer will always be zero.	$a + -a = 0$ $5 + -5 = 0$
Set	A specific group of numbers or objects	Set of integers: $\{... -3, -2, -1, 0, 1, 2, 3 ...\}$

Common Mathematics Symbols and Terms (cont.)

Absolute Value	The absolute value of a number can be considered as the distance between the number and zero on the number line. The absolute value of every number will be either positive or zero. Real numbers come in paired opposites, a and $-a$, that are the same distance from the origin but in opposite directions.	Absolute value of a: $\lvert a \rvert = a$ if a is positive $\lvert -a \rvert = a$ if a is negative $\lvert a \rvert = 0$ if a is 0 If 0 is the origin on the number line on the left, 3 is the absolute value of the pair -3 and +3 because they are both 3 marks from 0.
Expression	A certain number or variable, or numbers and variables, combined by operations such as addition, subtraction, multiplication, or division	$-3xy$ $2ab + b$ $2z + 4c + 2 - y$
Monomial Expression	A number, variable, or the product of a number and one or more variables raised to whole-number powers	a $\frac{1}{2}r$ $-3xy$
Binomial Expression	Has 2 unlike terms combined by an addition or subtraction sign. Sum of the number, variable, or product of a number and one or more variables raised to whole-number powers with only two terms	$2x - 9$ $2ab + b$ $x + 3$ $x - 7$
Polynomial Expression	Has 1, 2, 3, or more terms combined by an addition or subtraction sign. Sum of the number, variable, or product of a number and one or more variables raised to whole-number powers	$4a + 6$ $x^2 + 5 + 5x$ $z + a + b - a$ $2z + 4c + 2 - y$

Common Mathematics Symbols and Terms (cont.)

Function	The relation of one variable to another. The value of one variable depends on the value of the other variable.	*Example 1:* $d = 0.2t + 2$ *Example 2:*
	A relation in which each input number has one output number	
	A rule that pairs a number from one set with a number in a second set	
	Provides a description of a relationship between two variables, an input variable, and an output variable. The output variable depends on the input variable.	Each input value in the *x* column is paired with exactly one output value in the *y* column.
Ordered Pair	Describes a point on a graph. The first number in the pair tells the location on the *x*-axis, and the second tells the location of the point on the *y*-axis.	(3, 8) - three to the right of 0 on the *x*-axis; 8 up on the *y*-axis. The point is where these two intersect.
Relation	A set of ordered pairs where the first components of the ordered pair are the input values, and the second are the output values.	(5, 10)
Domain	Set of all input values to which the rule applies; (independent variables) the first number in an ordered pair	{(5, 6), (10, 7)} The set {5, 10} is the domain for this rule.
Range	Set of all output values to which the rule applies; (dependent variables) the second number in an ordered pair	{(5, 6), (10, 7)} The set {6, 7} is the range for this rule.
Function Notation	$f(x)$ or "*f* of *x*"	If *x* is the input variable, and you are looking for the functional value of $f(2)$ for the function of $f(x) = x^4 - 2$, substitute 2 for the *x* in this rule.
Comparison Property	Exactly one of these statements is true. $a < b \quad a = b \quad a > b$	$9 < 11 \quad 7 = 7 \quad -3 > -5$

The Example 2 table within the Function row:

x	y
-1	0
5	6
0	1
7	8

Common Mathematics Symbols and Terms (cont.)

Transitive Property	If $a < b$ and $b < c$, then $a < c$.	$3 < 10 < 12$
Addition Property	If $a < b$, then $a + c < b + c$	$4 < 6$ $\quad 4 + 2 < 6 + 2$
Multiplication Property	If $a < b$ and c is a positive number, then $ac < bc$. If $a < b$ and c is a negative number, then $ac > bc$.	$4 < 6$ $\quad 4(2) < 6(2)$ $4 < 6$ $\quad 4(-2) > 6(-2)$
Conjunction	A sentence formed by joining two sentences and the word *and*. A conjunction is true only when both sentences are true.	$x > -2$ and $x < 3$
Disjunction	A sentence formed by joining two sentences with the word *or*. A disjunction is only true if at least one of the sentences is true.	$x < 2$ or $x = 2$
Open Sentences	An equation or inequality that contains one or more variables.	$x < 9$ $x = 4 + y$
Solution Set	Set of all solutions for an open sentence	$x < 9$ Solution set: $\{8, 7, 6, \dots\}$
Constant	A number	$-3, \frac{1}{2}, 0$
Degree of a Variable	Number of times the variable is a factor	$3x^3$ $\quad$ Degree of x is 3 $2y^2$ $\quad$ Degree of y is 2
Degree of a Monomial	Sum of the degrees in the monomial	$3ab^3$ $\quad$ Degree of $3ab^3$ (1 for a + 3 for b) is 4
Similar Monomials Also called **Like Monomials**	Monomials that are alike or only the coefficients are different	ab^3 and $3ab^3$ are similar ab^2 and $3ab^3$ are not similar
Simplified Polynomial	Polynomial that has no two terms that are similar. The terms are usually arranged in order of decreasing degree of one of the variables.	$3x^3 + 2x^2 + 4x - 1$

Common Mathematics Symbols and Terms (cont.)

Degree of Polynomial	The greatest of the degrees of its terms after it has been simplified.	$3x^3 + 2x^2y^2 + 4x - 1$ $3x^3$ (degree is 3) + $2x^2y^2$ (degree is 4 because you add the 2 exponents) + $4x$ (degree is 1) $- 1$ (0 has no degree). The highest degree then is 4, so the degree of this polynomial is 4.
Prime Factorization	The process of writing a positive integer as a product of primes	$24 = 2 \bullet 2 \bullet 2 \bullet 3$
Greatest Common Factor (GCF)	Factor having the greatest degree and greatest constant factor	The greatest common factor of 6, 8, and 12 is 2.
Least Common Multiple (LCM)	The least common multiple of 2 or more integers is the least positive integer having each as a factor.	The least common multiple of 6, 10, and 12 is $60 = 2 \bullet 2 \bullet 3 \bullet 5$.
	The least common multiple of 2 or more monomials is the common multiple having the least degree and the least positive numerical coefficient.	The least common multiple of $2a$, $4a^3$, and $6a^2$ is $12a^3$.
	The least common multiple of 2 or more polynomials is the common multiple having the least degree and least positive constant factor.	The least common multiple of $3x(2 - y)^2$, $10x^3$, and $5x^2(2 - y)^2$ is $30x^3(2 - y)^2$.
Factor	Expressed as the product of two numbers or polynomials	$10x^2 - 90y^2 =$ $2 \bullet 5 \bullet (x - 3y) \bullet (x + 3y)$
Factor Set	Set from which numbers or polynomials are chosen as factors	The factor set for 14 is $\{(1)(14), (-1)(-14), (2)(7), (-2)(-7)\}$
Prime Number	An integer greater than 1 whose only positive factors are 1 and itself.	2, 3, 5, 7, etc.

Common Mathematics Symbols and Terms (cont.)

Repeating or Infinite Decimal	The quotient is a repeating decimal if the decimal repeats a number or block of numbers endlessly as a remainder	$\frac{4}{11} = 0.3636363636\ldots$ $\frac{37}{7} = 5.285714285714\ldots$
Finite or Terminating Decimal	The quotient is a finite or terminating decimal if there is no remainder	$\frac{53}{20} = 2.65$ $\frac{3}{32} = 0.09375$
Imaginary Numbers	Numbers bi where b is a nonzero real number are called pure imaginary numbers.	$x = \sqrt{-1} = \pm i.$
Complex Numbers	Real numbers are expanded to include imaginary numbers. When pure imaginary numbers are combined with real numbers, imaginary numbers of the form $a + bi$ $(b \neq 0)$ are the result.	$a + bi$ $(b \neq 0)$ $5 + 3\sqrt{-1}$
Real Numbers	Real numbers are a combination of all the number systems: natural numbers, whole numbers, integers, rational numbers, and irrational numbers.	$\frac{3}{4}$; 7; 6.8; -61; $0.\overline{27}$; 3,703; $\sqrt{3}$; -0.95
Irrational Numbers	Numbers that cannot be expressed as a ratio of two integers	$\sqrt{3}$
Rational Numbers	A number that can be expressed as the ratio of two integers	$\frac{1}{2}$
Completeness Property	Every real number has a decimal representation, and every decimal represents a real number.	$\frac{1}{2} = 0.5$
Quadratic Formula	Solutions for a quadratic equation $ax^2 + bx + c = 0$ if $a \neq 0$ $x = \dfrac{-b \pm \sqrt{b^2 - 4ac}}{2a}$ if $a \neq 0$	$x = \dfrac{-b \pm \sqrt{b^2 - 4ac}}{2a}$ if $a \neq 0$

Common Mathematics Symbols and Terms (cont.)

Quadratic Equation	Equations that include a term where the variable is raised to the second power (has an exponent of 2)	$ax^2 + bx + c = 0$
Discriminant	Discriminant shows whether or not the quadratic equation with integral coefficients has rational roots. If $D = 0$, there is a real double root. If $D > 0$, there are two different real roots. If $D < 0$, there are two complex conjugate roots.	$D = b^2 - 4ac$
Quadratic Function	Quadratic function is of the form, $f(x) = ax^2 + bx + c$, where a, b, and c are real numbers, and $a \neq 0$.	$f(x) = x^2 + 3x + 4$
Integral Coefficient	Integers as coefficients	$10x$; 10 is the coefficient
Conjugate	The conjugate of a binomial is another binomial having the same terms, but with the opposite sign between them. Solutions to quadratic equations with a negative discriminant always occur in conjugate pairs that are both complex numbers.	Examples of conjugates: $\sqrt{5} - 3$ and $\sqrt{5} + 3$ $7a + 3b$ and $7a - 3b$ $-2x + \sqrt{3}$ and $-2 - \sqrt{3}$ $1 + 2i$ and $1 - 2i$ are complex conjugate solutions to the equation: $x^2 - 2x + 5 = 0$

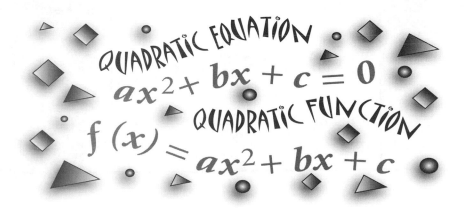

Algebra Rules and Laws

Rule	Description	Examples
Integer Subtraction Rule	For all integers a and b: $a - b = a + \text{-}b$	$12 - 5 = 12 + (\text{-}5)$
Equal Addition Rule	If equal quantities are added to each side of the equation, it does not change the root value of the equation.	$2y - 1 = 6$ $2y - 1 + 1 = 6 + 1$
Equal Subtraction Rule	If equal quantities are subtracted from each side of the equation, it does not change the root value of the equation.	$4x + 2 = 10$ $4x + 2 - 2 = 10 - 2$
Equal Multiplication Rule	If equal quantities are multiplied times each side of the equation, it does not change the root value of the equation.	$\dfrac{x}{6} = 3$ $(6)\dfrac{x}{6} = 3(6)$
Equal Division Rule	If equal quantities are divided into each side of the equation, it does not change the root value of the equation.	$4n = 8$ $\dfrac{4n}{4} = \dfrac{8}{4}$
Laws of Exponents	Let a and b be real numbers and n and m be positive integers: $a^m \bullet a^n = a^{m+n}$ $(ab)^m = a^m b^m$ $(a^m)^n = a^{mn}$ If $m > n$, $\dfrac{a^m}{a^n} = a^{m-n}$ If $n > m$, $\dfrac{a^m}{a^n} = \dfrac{1}{a^{n-m}}$	$x^2 \bullet x^3 = x^{2+3} = x^5$ $(xy)^2 = x^2 y^2$ $(c^2)^3 = c^{2(3)} = c^6$ $\dfrac{x^5}{x^3} = x^{5-3} = x^2$ $\dfrac{y^2}{y^5} = \dfrac{1}{y^{5-2}} = \dfrac{1}{y^3}$

Chapter 1: Solving Equations and Problems

Introduction to Solving Equations and Problems

Algebra uses expressions and equations. A numerical expression or numeral is a symbol or group of symbols used to represent a number. The value of a numerical expression is the number represented by the expression.

Simplify an expression by replacing it with the simplest or most common symbol having the same value. In order to simplify expressions, it is necessary to review some of the basic algebraic concepts.

Algebra uses equations to solve problems using numbers and/or variables. One of the major goals of algebra is to find unknown numbers. An equation is a mathematical sentence that uses numbers and variables to describe the relationship between two or more quantities. An equation is a mathematical statement that includes an equals sign. For example: $35 + 12 = 47$ is an equation. Variables are letters used to identify an unknown number. An example of an equation using variables is $2x + 7 = 4$. There are many kinds of equations, but the most commonly used in algebra are linear and quadratic equations. This section covers strategies for simplifying algebraic expressions, algebraic equations with one variable, changing word problems into algebraic symbols, and using algebraic equations to solve problems.

Concepts of Solving Equations and Problems

1. Simplifying Expressions
2. Solving Equations With One Variable
3. Words Into Symbols
4. Problem Solving With Equations

Explanation of the Concepts of Solving Equations and Problems

1 Simplifying Expressions

A mathematical sentence or algebraic expression is a symbol or group of symbols used to represent a number. The value of an expression is the number represented by the expression when the value of the variables is known.

Algebraic expressions can be simplified by using the rules for order of operation. Mathematicians have a specific order to be used in solving mathematical problems.

Chapter 1: Solving Equations and Problems (cont.)

The order of operation is:

Step **1**:	Do what is inside the parentheses.
Step **2**:	Compute the value of the exponents.
Step **3**:	Multiply and/or divide.
Step **4**:	Add and/or subtract.

Order of Operations

Example of Simplifying Algebraic Expressions:

Problem:	$3(4 + 3)$	
Step 1:	Do what is inside the parentheses.	$(4 + 3) = 7$
Step 2:	Substitute the 7 for $(4 + 3)$.	$3(7)$
Step 3:	Compute the value of the exponents.	No exponents
Step 4:	Multiply and/or divide.	$3(7) = 21$

② Solving Equations With One Variable

An equation is a mathematical sentence that uses numbers and/or variables to describe the relationship between two or more quantities. Sometimes you can look at an equation and guess what the number is. Sometimes you may have to solve the equation by using the principles of algebra. Equations can be solved by: 1) Simplifying each side of the equation, 2) Using addition and/or subtraction to solve equations, and 3) Using multiplication and/or division.

Examples of Simplifying Each Side of the Equation:

| **Problem:** | $7b = 5(6 + 1)$ |
| **Step 1:** | Simplify each side of the equation.
The left side is already simplified.
The right side can be simplified. $(6 + 1) = 7$
Substitute 7 for $(6 + 1)$.
Multiply $5(7) = 35$.
Substitute 35 for $5(6 + 1)$. $7b = 35$
The equation is simplified, so it can now be solved. |

Chapter 1: Solving Equations and Problems (cont.)

Problem: $4x + 2x - 7 + 9 + x = 5x - x$

Step 1: Simplify each side of the equation.
Simplify the left side.
Combine all terms with the same variable. $4x + 2x + x = 7x$
Combine all numbers on the left side. $-7 + 9 = 2$
Simplified, the left side is $7x + 2$.

Step 2: Simplify the right side.
Combine the terms with the same variables. $5x - x = 4x$
Simplified, the right side is $4x$.

Step 3: Substitute the simplified left and right sides. $7x + 2 = 4x$
The equation is simplified, so it can be solved.

To solve the simplified equations with one variable by addition and subtraction, first move the variables to one side of the equation and the numbers to the other side of the equation by adding or subtracting. If an equation is a true sentence, then the left side is equal to the right side of the equation. If you add or subtract the same number to each side of the equation, the equation is still true.

Example of Simplifying Equations With One Variable by Addition and Subtraction:

Problem: $x - 4 = 9$

Step 1: Equation is simplified.

Step 2: Get the variable on one side and the numbers on the other.
Variables are on one side.
The number -4 must be moved to the other side.
Remember that as long as you do the same thing to both sides of the equation, it does not change the value of the equation. So if we add 4 to both sides of the equation, it will move the four to the other side.
$x - 4 + 4 = 9 + 4$

Answer: Combine the terms. $x = 13$

Chapter 1: Solving Equations and Problems (cont.)

Examples of Simplifying Equations With One Variable by Multiplication and Division:

Problem: $7b = 5(6 + 1)$

Step 1:   Simplify each side of the equation. From a previous example, we know this equation can be simplified to $7b = 35$.

Step 2:   Solve the equation. Multiply and/or divide. Remember that as long as you do the same thing to both sides of the equation, it does not change the value of the equation. Divide both sides by 7.

$$\frac{7b}{7} = \frac{35}{7}$$

Answer: $b = 5$

Problem: $4x + 2x - 7 + 9 + x = 5x - x$

Step 1:   Simplify each side of the equation. From a previous example, we know this equation can be simplified to $7x + 2 = 4x$.

Step 2:   Get the variables on one side of the equation and the numbers on the other side. Add and/or subtract.
$7x + 2 - 2 = 4x - 2$
$7x - 4x = 4x - 2 - 4x$
$3x = \text{-}2$

Step 3:   Multiply and/or divide. Divide both sides by 3.

$$\frac{3x}{3} = \frac{\text{-}2}{3}$$

Answer: $x = \text{-}\frac{2}{3}$

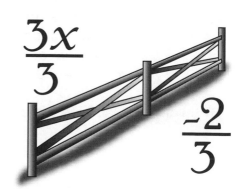

Chapter 1: Solving Equations and Problems (cont.)

 Words Into Symbols

Word problems describe relationships between numbers. If you change the relationships of the numbers into an equation, you can solve the problem by solving the equation. Word problems can be solved by changing some of the words in the phrase or sentence into numbers and/or symbols and putting them into algebraic expressions.

Example of Changing Word Phrases Into Algebraic Expressions:

"five more than three times the number"

Use n for the variable.
"five more" is represented by $+ 5$.
"three times the number" is represented by $3 \quad n$ or $3n$.
So the expression representing "five more than three times the number" is $3n + 5$.

Example of Changing Sentences Into Algebraic Expressions:

"If a runner runs at x miles/hour, what would her speed be if she ran 2 miles per hour slower?"

"speed" is represented by x.
"2 miles an hour slower" is represented by $- 2$.
So the runner's speed could be represented by the algebraic expression $x - 2$.

Example of Using a Variable as an Unknown and Writing an Equation to Represent the Situation:

Your class has 23 students. The number of boys is 4 less than two times the girls. How would you write an algebraic equation to represent this?

Choose a variable to represent the unknown, the number of girls. Girls = g
Write an expression for the number of boys in terms of the variable.
Boys are represented by $2g - 4$.
Write the equation that represents the situation. There are 23 students in the class.
$g + (2g - 4) = 23$ or $3g - 4 = 23$

Chapter 1: Solving Equations and Problems (cont.)

4 Problem Solving With Equations

In solving problems with equations, you need to translate the relationship described in the word problem into an equation. Start by reading the problem carefully and asking what you are trying to find out. Choose a variable and use it with the given facts to represent the numbers in the problem. Write out a word equation to represent the relationship between the numbers. This should give you an algebraic equation that can be solved. Check your results.

Example of Problem Solving With Equations:

Tickets to a major league game were $100 for a box seat and $50 for a bleacher seat. There were 1,000 more bleacher seats sold than box seats. If the total ticket sales were $62,000, how many of each ticket were sold?

Step 1: What are you trying to find out? "How many of each ticket were sold?"

Step 2: Choose a variable to represent the relationship. Let b represent the number of box seats.

Step 3: Write a word equation to represent the relationship.
Money from the Box Tickets Sold + Money from the Bleacher Tickets Sold = Total Sales

Step 4: Write it out as an algebraic equation. $\$100\ b + \$50(b + 1{,}000) = \$62{,}000$

Step 5: Simplify. $100b + 50b + 50{,}000 = 62{,}000$

Step 6: Combine the same variables. $150b + 50{,}000 = 62{,}000$

Step 7: Solve the equation by subtraction to get the variables on one side and the numbers on the other side.
$150b + 50{,}000 - 50{,}000 = 62{,}000 - 50{,}000$
$150b = 12{,}000$
$$\frac{150b}{150} = \frac{12{,}000}{150}$$
$b = 80$ box seats were sold.

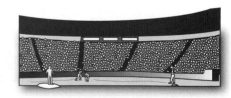

Answer: There were 80 box seats sold. The number of bleacher seats is 1,000 more than the box seats. Bleacher seats = $b + 1{,}000$
The number of bleacher seats is $80 + 1{,}000 = 1{,}080$.

Check your answer: Substitute the numbers in the original equation.
Money from the Box Tickets Sold + Money from the Bleacher Tickets Sold = Total Sales. $\$100\ b + \$50(b + 1{,}000) = \$62{,}000$
Substitute the 80 for number of box seats. $\$150(80) + \$50(80 + 1{,}000) = \$62{,}000$

Name: _____ Date: _____

Chapter 1: Solving Equations and Problems (cont.)

Practice: Solving Equations and Problems

Simplifying Expressions
Simplify the following expressions.

1. 4 $(2 + 2) - 1$

2. $(5 - 3)^2(2 - 1)$

3. $5x - (6 - 3) + 7$

Simplify each side of the equation.

4. $4a + 5a - 2 = 5 + 3 - 1$

5. $3x - 2x + x - 4 + 3 - 2 = 0$

6. $3(x + 5) = 0$

7. $3x - 2x = 6 - 9$

8. $3x + 4x = 6(2x + 1)$

Solving Equations With One Variable
Simplify and solve the equations in questions 9–13.

9. $4a + 5a - 2 = 5 + 3 - 1$

10. $3x - 2x + x - 4 + 3 - 2 = 0$

11. $3(x + 5) = 0$

12. $3x - 2x = 6 - 9$

13. $3x + 4x = 6(2x + 1)$

Chapter 1: Solving Equations and Problems (cont.)

Words Into Symbols

For questions 14–19, express each phrase or sentence in symbols in the simplest form in terms of the given variable.

14. The cube of a number decreased by that number _____

15. Three times the sum of a number and 7 _____

16. What is the area of a tabletop that is twice as long as it is wide? _____

17. What is the price of a pencil if the price of 24 pencils is $1.00? _____

18. Yuki has n DVDs. If she has 13 fewer than Frieda, and Frieda has 80 DVDs, then how many does Yuki have?

    _____

19. If a car traveled for 3 hours at r mph and increased the speed by 10 mph and traveled for 1 more hour, how far did the car travel?

    _____

For questions 20–21, choose a variable to represent the unknown number and write an equation to describe a given situation.

20. The eighth grade class has 75 students. The number of girls is 6 less than twice the number of boys.

    _____

21. Ian bought a pair of jeans at the regular price. When the jeans went on sale, he purchased 3 more pairs that were $5 off of the regular price. He spent a total of $50 for 4 pairs of jeans.

    _____

Problem Solving With Equations

Change this word problem into a mathematical equation and solve.

22. Tara receives an annual return of $332 from $5,000 invested at a simple interest. How much is the interest rate? (Interest = amount invested   interest rate).

    _____

Chapter 1: Solving Equations and Problems (cont.)

Summary of Solving Equations and Problems

To simplify expressions, use the following order for operations:
1. Simplify the expression within each grouping symbol, working outward from the innermost group.
2. Simplify the powers.
3. Perform multiplication and division from left to right.
4. Perform addition and subtraction in order from left to right.

Simplify an expression by replacing it by the simplest or most common symbol having the same value. To simplify an algebraic expression, replace each variable in an expression by a given value and simplify the results.

To solve the simplified equations with one variable by addition and subtraction, first move the variables to one side of the equation and the numbers to the other side of the equation by adding or subtracting.

Word problems describe relationships between numbers. If you change the relationships of the numbers into an equation, you can solve the problem by solving the equation. Word problems can be solved by changing some of the words in the phrase or sentence into numbers and/or symbols and putting them into algebraic expressions.

In solving problems with equations, you need to translate the relationship described in the word problem into an equation. Start by reading the problem carefully and asking what you are trying to find out. Choose a variable and use it with the given facts to represent the numbers in the problem. Write out a word equation to represent the relationship between the numbers. Then write the word equation as an algebraic equation and solve it. Check your results.

Tips to Remember

Two hints will help change the word problems into mathematical statements. Usually the words *equals, is, are, was,* and *were* in sentences are changed to an equals sign (=). The second hint is to use a letter to represent an unknown number (a variable).

Real Life Applications of Solving Equations and Problems

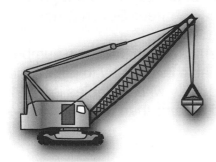

Changing words into algebraic expressions can be used to solve problems in science. To find the amount of work done by a machine, the formula used is "work equals the force times the distance." If you represent the work with the variable W, force with f, and distance with d, the formula becomes $W = f \cdot d$. Solving problems with equations can also be used to determine interest rates on investments.

Chapter 2: Inequalities

Introduction to Inequalities

Equations are sentences in which both sides are equal and are connected by an equals sign (=). This section will examine inequalities. Operations on inequalities are similar to the operations used for equalities. An inequality is a sentence in which one side of the expression is greater than or less than the other side.

Inequalities Concepts

1 Introduction to Inequalities

2 Graphing Inequalities

3 Solving Inequalities

4 Working With Absolute Values

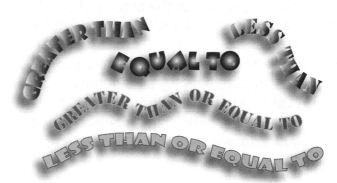

Explanations of Concepts of Inequalities

1 **Introduction to Inequalities**

An inequality is a sentence in which one side of the expression is greater than or less than the other side. Symbols for inequalities include:

Greater than $>$
Less than $<$
Greater than or equal to $\geq$
Less than or equal to $\leq$

Inequalities can be true or false. An example of a true inequality is $4 > 2$. This is read "four is greater than two." Four is a larger number than two, so the statement is true. The inequality $-3 \geq -6$ is also a true statement. Negative three is greater than or equal to negative six. Since the negative three is greater than the negative six, the statement is true. $2 < 10$ is read "two is less than ten." This statement is also true because two is less than ten. There are also inequalities that are not true. $5 > 12$ or "five is greater than twelve" is not true because five is not greater than twelve. The inequality $7 \leq 3$ means "seven is less than or equal to three." Seven is not less than three, and it is not equal to three, so the statement $7 \leq 3$ is not true.

Inequalities can also contain variables. Remember that a variable is an unknown number that is represented by a letter. In algebra, if an inequality has a variable in it, we try to determine the values that might make it true or false. An example of an inequality with variables is $x > 4$. This is read "x is greater than four." If the number x represents is greater than four, it is a true statement. If it is less than four, the statement is false.

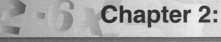

Chapter 2: Inequalities (cont.)

2 Graphing Inequalities

Inequalities with a variable can be shown on a graph or number line. An inequality can be graphed in three steps.

Step 1:   Locate the number on the number line.

Step 2:   Check to see if the inequality sign is < (is less than), > (greater than), ≤ (less than or equal to), or ≥ (greater than or equal to).

Step 3:   If it is greater than (>) or greater than or equal to (≥), shade the number line to the right of the number. If it is less than (<) or less than or equal to (≤), shade the number line to the left of the number. When the inequality is > or <, use an empty circle on the number since it has to be greater or less than the number itself. Place a shaded circle on the number if it is ≤ or ≥ to show that the number is included.

Examples of Graphing > Inequalities:

$x > 3$

Step 1:   Locate the number on the number line.

Step 2:   Check the sign. The sign is >.

Step 3:   As it is >, do not include the number.

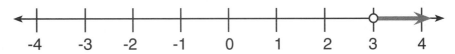

Examples of Graphing ≥ Inequalities:

$x ≥ 3$

Step 1:   Locate the number on the number line.

Step 2:   Check the sign. The sign is ≥.

Step 3:   As it is ≥, graph to the right of the number and include the number.

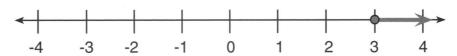

Chapter 2: Inequalities (cont.)

Examples of Graphing < Inequalities:

$x < 3$

Step **1**:	Locate the number on the number line.
Step **2**:	Check the sign. The sign is <.
Step **3**:	As it is <, graph to the left of the number and do not include the number.

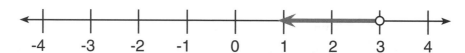

Examples of Graphing ≤ Inequalities:

$x \leq 3$

Step **1**:	Locate the number on the number line.
Step **2**:	Check the sign. The sign is ≤.
Step **3**:	As it is ≤, graph to the left of the number and include the number.

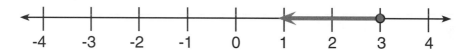

③ Solving Inequalities

Equations can be solved by: 1) Simplifying each side of the equation, 2) Using addition and/or subtraction to solve equations, and 3) Using multiplication and/or division. Solving inequalities requires the same steps as solving equations with two exceptions. When the answers to an inequality are found, they can be graphed on a number line, since there is usually more than one answer. The other difference is if you multiply or divide by a negative number, the direction of the inequality reverses. You can check your work by changing the inequality sign to an equals sign and solving the equation using one of the numbers included on your graph in place of the variable. You can check the direction of the arrow by substituting zero for the variable.

Chapter 2: Inequalities (cont.)

Example of Solving Inequalities With One Variable:

$x > -2$

Step 1: Simplify each side of the inequality.
$x > -2$ is already simplified.

Step 2: Using addition and/or subtraction and multiplication and/or division does not apply, since the inequality is already simplified.

Step 3: Graphing the inequality:

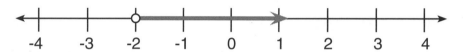

Step 4: Checking the inequality:
Substitute one of the numbers included for the variable.
-1 > -2   This statement is true.
Substitute zero for the variable. 0 > -2   This is also true.
Zero is included, so the direction is correct.

To solve more complex inequalities, use methods similar to solving equations. These methods are based on the properties of order for real numbers. Properties of order include comparison property, transitive property, addition property, and multiplication property. Assuming that the variables a, b, and c are any real numbers, the **comparison property** states that exactly one of the following statements is true $a < b$, $a = b$, or $a > b$. The **transitive property** for less than/greater than, assuming that the variables a, b, and c are any real numbers, states that if $a < b$ and $b < c$ then $a < c$, and if $a > b$ and $b > c$ then $a > c$. Assuming that the variables a, b, and c are any real numbers, the **addition property** states that if $a < b$, then $a + c < b + c$. Again assuming that the variables a, b, and c are any real numbers, the **multiplication property** states that if $a < b$ and c is positive, then $ac < bc$, and if $a < b$ and c is a negative number, then $ac > bc$.

Example of Solving More Complex Inequalities With One Variable:

$2(x - 1) > 4$

Step 1: Simplify each side of the inequality.
$2x - 2 > 4$

Step 2: Use addition and/or subtraction.
$2x - 2 + 2 > 4 + 2$
$2x > 6$

Step 3: Use multiplication and/or division.
$\dfrac{2x}{2} > \dfrac{6}{2}$

Answer: $x > 3$

27

Chapter 2: Inequalities (cont.)

Checking the problem:	Pick a number that makes the statement true. 5 > 3 makes the statement true.

Substitute 5 in the original inequality and see if it makes the statement true.

$2(x - 1) > 4$
$2(5 - 1) > 4$
$3(4) > 4$
$12 > 4$

The statement is true, so the inequality solution is correct.

Graphing the inequality:

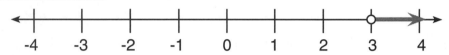

Checking the inequality graph:

$x > 3$
Substitute one of the numbers included for the variable. 4 > 3
This statement is true.
Substitute zero for the variable. 0 > 3 This is not true, so zero is not included, and the direction of the arrow is correct.

Example of Solving Inequalities With One Variable With Negative Numbers:

$2x - 5x + 4 \leq 10$

Step 1:	Simplify each side of the inequality. $-3x + 4 \leq 10$
Step 2:	Use addition and/or subtraction. $-3x + 4 - 4 \leq 10 - 4$ $-3x \leq 6$
Step 3:	Use multiplication and/or division. $\dfrac{-3x}{-3} \leq \dfrac{6}{-3}$
Answer:	$x \geq -2$ (When you multiply or divide by a negative number, reverse the direction of the inequality.)

28

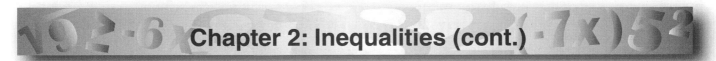

Chapter 2: Inequalities (cont.)

Checking the problem:

Pick a number that makes the statement true. $3 \geq -2$ makes the statement true.
Substitute 3 in the original inequality and see if it makes the statement true.
$-3x + 4 \leq 10$
$-3(3) + 4 \leq 10$
$-9 + 4 \leq 10$
$-5 \leq 10$ The statement is true, so the solution is correct.

Graphing the inequality:

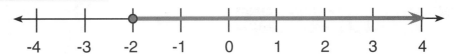

Checking the inequality graph:

$x \geq -2$
Substitute one of the numbers included for the variable. $2 \geq -2$
This statement is true.
Substitute zero for the variable. $0 \geq -2$ This statement is true, so zero is included, and the direction of the arrow is correct.

Combined inequalities are formed when two inequalities are combined with the words *and* or *or*. A **conjunction** is a sentence formed by joining two sentences with the word *and*. A conjunction is true only when both sentences are true. A **disjunction** is a sentence formed by joining two sentences with the word *or*. A disjunction is true if at least one of the sentences is true.

Example of Solving a Conjunction:

A conjunction is formed when two inequalities are joined by the word *and*.
$x > -2$ and $x < 3$

Step 1:   Simplify each side of the inequality. Both inequalities are simplified.

Step 2:   Use addition and/or subtraction. Both inequalities are simplified.

Step 3:   Use multiplication and/or division. Both inequalities are simplified.

Checking the solution is not necessary, since both inequalities are already simplified.

Graphing the inequality:

Chapter 2: Inequalities (cont.)

Checking the conjunction graph:

$x > -2$ and $x < 3$
Substitute one of the numbers included on the graph for the variable.
$2 > -2$ and $2 < 3$ Both statements are true.
Substitute zero for the variable. $0 > -2$ and $0 < 3$ Both statements are true, so zero is included, and the graph correctly represents this conjunction.

The conjunction is true because both statements are true.

Example of Solving a Disjunction:

A disjunction is formed when two inequalities are joined by the word *or.*
$x < 2$ or $x = 2$

Step 1: Simplify each side of the inequality. Both inequalities are simplified.

Step 2: Use addition and/or subtraction. Both inequalities are simplified.

Step 3: Use multiplication and/or division. Both inequalities are simplified.

Checking the solution is not necessary since both inequalities are already simplified.

Graphing the inequality:

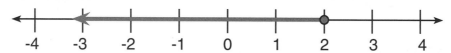

Checking the disjunction:

$x < 2$ or $x = 2$
Substitute one of the numbers included for the variable. $-3 < 2$ or $-3 = 2$
$-3 < 2$ is true, $-3 = 2$ is false.
Substitute zero for the variable. $0 < 2$ or $0 = 2$
$0 < 2$ is true, $0 = 2$ is false.

The disjunction is true because at least one statement is true.

Chapter 2: Inequalities (cont.)

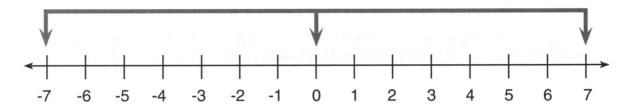

4 **Working With Absolute Values**

The **absolute value** of a number *n* is the answer to the question "how far from zero is *n* on the number line?" For example, the absolute value of 7, shown symbolically as |7|, would be 7. The absolute value of |-7| is also 7. Examine the number line below. The distance from 0 to 7 is 7 marks and from 0 to -7 is also 7 marks.

-7 -6 -5 -4 -3 -2 -1 0 1 2 3 4 5 6 7

In general, if the number is positive, then the absolute value is the number itself. If it is a negative number, the absolute value is the additive inverse or opposite of that number. The absolute value of a quantity is always positive or 0 because it represents a distance. The absolute value of *x* is written |*x*|.

Solving open sentences involving absolute value can be done by first writing an equivalent disjunction or conjunction.

Example of Solving Sentences With Absolute Values—Disjunction:

$|3x - 2| = 8$

Equivalent Sentence

$3x - 2 = 8$ or $3x - 2 = -8$

Step 1:   Simplify each side of the equation.
$3x - 2 = 8$ or $3x - 2 = -8$

Step 2:   Use addition and/or subtraction.
$3x - 2 = 8$ or $3x - 2 = -8$
$3x - 2 + 2 = 8 + 2$ or $3x - 2 + 2 = -8 + 2$
$3x = 10$ or $3x = -6$

Step 3:   Use multiplication and/or division.
$$\frac{3x}{3} = \frac{10}{3}$$ or $$\frac{3x}{3} = \frac{-6}{3}$$

Answers: $x = \frac{10}{3}$ or $x = -2$

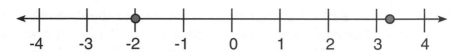

Graphing:

The solution set is $\{ -2, \frac{10}{3} \}$

Example of Solving Sentences With Absolute Values—Conjunction:

$|3 - 2x| < 5$

Equivalent Sentence

$3 - 2x < 5$ and $3 - 2x > -5$ (Some texts write this as $-5 < 3 - 2x < 5$.)

Step 1:   Simplify each side of the equation.
$3 - 2x < 5$ and $3 - 2x > -5$

Step 2:   Use addition and/or subtraction.
$3 - 2x < 5$ and $3 - 2x > -5$
$3 - 2x - 3 < 5 - 3$ $3 - 2x - 3 > -5 - 3$
$-2x < 2$ $-2x > -8$

Step 3:   Use multiplication and/or division.
$\dfrac{-2x}{-2} > \dfrac{2}{-2}$ and $\dfrac{-2x}{-2} < \dfrac{-8}{-2}$

When you multiply or divide both numbers by a negative number, the inequality reverses direction.

Answers: $x > -1$ and $x < 4$

Graphing:

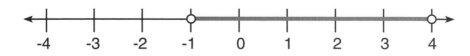

The solution set is $x > -1$ and $x < 4$ or written as $\{x : -1 < x < 4\}$.

32

Name: _____ Date: _____

Chapter 2: Inequalities (cont.)

Practice: Inequalities

For questions 1–5, identify which inequalities are true and which are false.

1. $3 > 7$ _____

2. $6 \geq 8$ _____

3. $6 \leq 6$ _____

4. $0 < -6$ _____

5. $-6 \leq -1$ _____

For questions 6–8, write the statement in words, and then identify the numbers that would make the inequality true.

6. $a < 5$ Statement in words: _____

Numbers that make the inequality true: _____

7. $c \geq 2$ Statement in words: _____

Numbers that make the inequality true: _____

8. $x \leq 0$ Statement in words: _____

Numbers that make the inequality true: _____

Graphing Inequalities

For questions 9–12, graph the inequalities on a number line.

9. $n \leq 10$
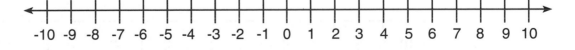

10. $b \geq -4$
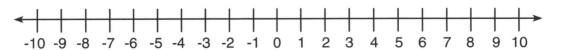

11. $x < -\frac{3}{4}$
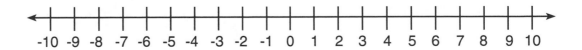

12. $x > 4$
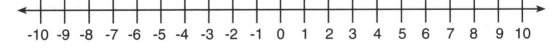

33

Name: _____ Date: _____

Chapter 2: Inequalities (cont.)

Solving Inequalities

For questions 13–16, solve the inequalities and check your answers.

13. $3x > 9$

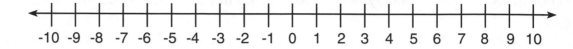

14. $\frac{1}{2}x \leq 4$

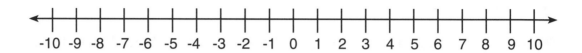

15. $2(y + 1) + 3 < y$

16. $-\frac{3}{2}x < -12$

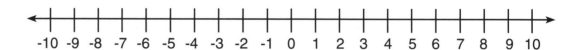

Conjunctions and Disjunctions

For questions 17–18, solve the inequalities and tell which one is an example of a conjunction and which is a disjunction and why.

17. $3 < 2x + 5$ and $2x + 5 \leq 15$

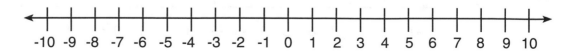

Name: _____ Date: _____

Chapter 2: Inequalities (cont.)

18. $7 - 2y \leq 1$ or $3y + 10 < 4 - y$

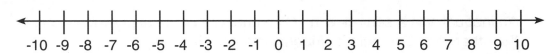

For questions 19–20, match the open sentences with the correct graphs. Place the letter of the open sentence on the blank next to the correct graph.

    a. $x \leq -2$ or $x > 3$ b. $x \geq -2$ and $x < 3$

19. _____

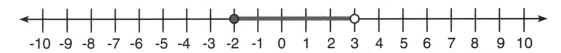

20. _____

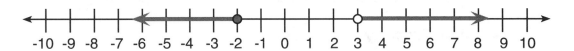

Working With Absolute Values

For question 21, determine the equivalent sentences, solve each inequality, graph the inequalities, and find the solution set.

21. $|3t - 1| > 2$

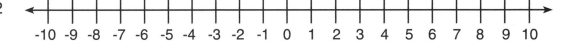

35

Chapter 2: Inequalities (cont.)

Summary of Inequalities

- An inequality is a sentence in which one side of the expression is greater than or less than the other side. Symbols for inequalities include:
    Greater than   >
    Less than   <
    Greater than or equal to   ≥
    Less than or equal to   ≤

- Inequalities can be true or false.

- Assume that the variables a, b, and c are any real numbers.

    Comparison Property
        Exactly one of the following statements is true:
        $a < b$ $a = b$ $a > b$.

    Transitive Property
        If $a < b$ and $b < c$, then $a < c$.

    Addition Property
        If $a < b$, then $a + c < b + c$.

    Multiplication Property
        If $a < b$ and c is positive, then $ac < bc$.
        If $a < b$ and c is a negative number, then $ac > bc$.

Tip to Remember

If you multiply or divide by a negative number, the direction of the inequality reverses.

Real Life Applications of Inequalities

Inequalities could be used to compare cell phone plans and examine which is the best plan for the monthly fees.

Chapter 3: Linear Equations and Inequalities

Introduction to the Concepts of Linear Equations and Inequalities

A linear equation in one variable is any equation that can be put into the general form, $ax + b = 0$ where a and b can be any real numbers. When you solve an equation, you are trying to find a number to replace the variable to make the statement true. Like the linear equations, the solution for linear inequalities is an ordered pair of numbers that makes the inequality true or satisfies the inequality.

Linear Equations and Inequalities Concepts

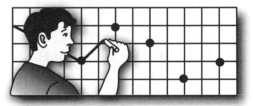

1. Linear Equations and Graphs
2. Linear Equations in Two Variables
3. Linear Inequalities in Two Variables
4. Linear Systems

Explanations of the Concepts of Linear Equations and Inequalities

1. Linear Equations and Graphs

There are four rules for solving any type of equation.

1. **Equal Additions Rule**

   If the same number is added to each side of an equation, the solutions of the original equation are the solutions of the new equation.

   Add equal quantities to each side of the equation. $x - 6 = 18$
   Add the same quantity to each side. $x - 6 + 6 = 18 + 6$
   $x = 24$
   Check the answer by substituting the number for x in the original equation.
   $24 - 6 = 18$

2. **Equal Subtraction Rule**

   If the same number is subtracted from each side of an equation, the solutions of the original equation are the solutions of the new equation.

   Subtract equal quantities from each side of the equation. $x + 2 = 11$
   Subtract the same quantity from each side of the equation. $x + 2 - 2 = 11 - 2$
   $x = 9$
   Check the answer by substituting the number for x in the original equation.
   $9 + 2 = 11$

Chapter 3: Linear Equations and Inequalities (cont.)

3. Equal Multiplication Rule

If each side of an equation is multiplied by the same number, the solutions of the original equation are the solutions of the new equation.

Multiply each side by the same quantity. $\frac{1}{4}y = 5$

The reciprocal of $\frac{1}{4}$ is 4, so multiply each side by 4. $\frac{1}{4}y \cdot 4 = 5 \cdot 4$
$y = 20$

Check the answer by substituting the number for y in the original equation.
$\frac{1}{4} \cdot 20 = 5$
$\frac{1}{4} \cdot \frac{20}{1} = \frac{20}{4} = 5$

4. Equal Division Rule

If each side of an equation is divided by the same non-zero number, the solutions of the original equation are the solutions of the new equation.

Divide each side by the same quantity. $5a = 120$
Divide each side by the same quantity. $\frac{5a}{5} = \frac{120}{5}$

$a = 24$
Check the answer by substituting the number for a in the original equation.
$5 \cdot 24 = 120$

Example of Using Linear Equations to Solve Problems:

$3x + 9 = 108$

Step 1:   Simplify using rules for order of operation.

Step 2:   Subtract the same number from both sides.
$3x + 9 - 9 = 108 - 9$
$3x = 99$

Step 3:   Divide each side by the same number.
$\frac{3x}{3} = \frac{99}{3}$

Answer: $x = 33$

Check the answer: $3(33) + 9 =$
$99 + 9 = 108$

Chapter 3: Linear Equations and Inequalities (cont.)

Example of Using Linear Equations to Solve Problems:

☐ Simplify each side of the equation using the rules for the order of operation.
☐ What do you need to do to find out what the variable is? There are two possible steps: 1) Add and/or subtract the same number and/or variable from both sides of the equation. 2) Multiply and/or divide both sides of the equation by the same number.
☐ Check your work using the answer.

If you run up 6 flights of stairs from the first floor of a tall building and walk down two flights, what floor are you on?

Identify the information that you already know.   Ran up 6 flights +6
                                                 Came down 2 flights -2

Information that you do not know x = current floor
Write the problem as an equation.   +6 + (-2) = x
Solve the equation.   +6 + (-2) = +4

➋ Linear Equations in Two Variables

The equations above were all open sentences in one variable. Equations and inequalities can also be open sentences in two variables, such as $9x + 3y = 15$ and $2x - y \geq 6$. There will be a pair of numbers for the solution. The pairs are called **ordered pairs** because there will be one value of x and one value of y that will make the statement true. The **solution set** is the set of all ordered pairs of numbers that satisfy the sentence or make it true.

Example of Finding the Solution Set:

Solve the equation $9x + 2y = 15$ if x is {-1, 0, 1, 2, 3}.

Problem: $9x + 2y = 15$

Step 1:   Simplify both sides of the equation. Both sides are simplified.

Step 2:   Use addition and/or subtraction.
$9x - 9x + 2y = 15 - 9x$
$2y = 15 - 9x$

Step 3:   Use multiplication and/or division.
$$\frac{2y}{2} = \frac{15 - 9x}{2} \qquad\qquad y = \frac{15 - 9x}{2}$$

Chapter 3: Linear Equations and Inequalities (cont.)

Step 4:   Using this equation, find the values of y.

If $x = -1$

$y = \dfrac{15 - 9(-1)}{2}$

$y = \dfrac{15 + 9}{2}$

$y = \dfrac{24}{2}$

$y = 12$

x	y	Solution Set
-1	12	(-1, 12)
0	$\frac{15}{2}$	$(0, \frac{15}{2})$
1	3	(1, 3)
2	$-\frac{3}{2}$	$(2, -\frac{3}{2})$
3	-6	(3, -6)

If $x = 0$

$y = \dfrac{15 - 9(0)}{2}$

$y = \dfrac{15 - 0}{2}$

$y = \dfrac{15}{2}$

If $x = 1$

$y = \dfrac{15 - 9(1)}{2}$

$y = \dfrac{15 - 9}{2}$

$y = \dfrac{6}{2}$

$y = 3$

If $x = 2$

$y = \dfrac{15 - 9(2)}{2}$

$y = \dfrac{15 - 18}{2}$

$y = \dfrac{-3}{2}$

If $x = 3$

$y = \dfrac{15 - 9(3)}{2}$

$y = \dfrac{15 - 27}{2}$

$y = \dfrac{-12}{2}$

$y = -6$

The solution set then is $\{(-1, 12), (0, \frac{15}{2}), (1, 3), (2, -\frac{3}{2}), (3, -6)\}$

A **coordinate plane** can be used to show number relationships of the ordered pairs that were just identified in the problem above. The notion of using a grid or a coordinate system to represent information was first envisioned and used by the mathematician René Descartes. For this reason, it is sometimes referred to as the **Cartesian coordinate system**. In the figure on the next page, a typical representation of this grid system, or coordinate plane, is shown. Notice that it works by putting two number lines together. The number line that measures

Chapter 3: Linear Equations and Inequalities (cont.)

distance from left to right (horizontally), moving from negative number values to positive number values, is called the **x-axis**. This *x*-axis is essentially the number line discussed and used in representing the real number system in earlier sections of this worktext. The number line that measures distance from bottom to top (vertically), moving from negative values to positive values, is called the **y-axis**.

By breaking up the plane using these two axes, the plane is divided into four sections or quarters, called **quadrants**. The four quadrants are typically labeled using Roman numerals (I, II, III, and IV) and are numbered moving in a counterclockwise direction from the upper right.

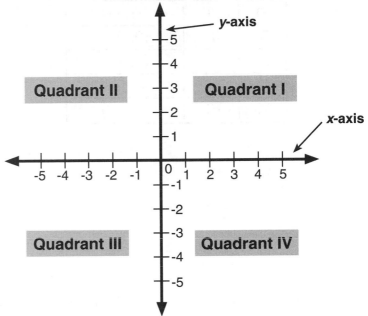

To mark a location on the coordinate plane means to plot a point and requires that two numbers be used. The two numbers form what is known as an **ordered pair**. An ordered pair is shown by using parentheses to enclose the pair of numbers with the numbers separated by a comma. For example, (-2, 5) is an ordered pair. The first number in the pair, -2, indicates how far right or left to move along the *x*-axis. Since it is a negative 2, we move left two units. The second number in the pair, 5, indicates how far up or down to move along the *y*-axis. Since it is positive 5, we move up five units and place a point in that location. Always start from the intersection point for the two number lines. The point that marks the intersection of the *x*- and *y*-axes is called the **origin** and is denoted with the ordered pair (0, 0).

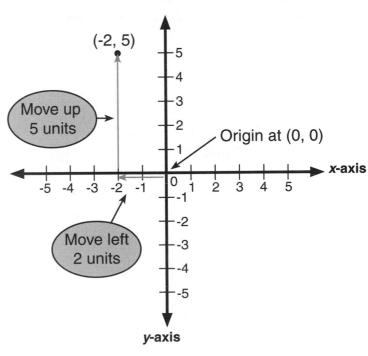

41

Chapter 3: Linear Equations and Inequalities (cont.)

Consider the equation $x - y = 0$ if $x = \{-1, 0, 1, 5, -6\}$. The ordered pairs that will make this statement true are in the table below. These ordered pairs are shown on the graph.

x	y	Solution Set
-1	-1	(-1, -1)
0	0	(0, 0)
1	1	(1, 1)
5	5	(5, 5)
-6	-6	(-6, -6)

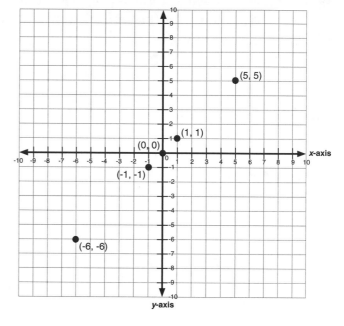

In the graph below, the points plotted in the graph above were connected together, and they appear to be in a line. Using this line, other possible solutions for this equation can be found.

Using the graph below, it appears that if $x = -8$, then y would be a -8. To find out if your answer is correct, substitute the values for x and y in the original equation. $x - y = 0$

$x - y = 0$
$-8 - (-8) = 0$
$-8 + 8 = 0$
$0 = 0$
So (-8, -8) would be another plot point in this set.

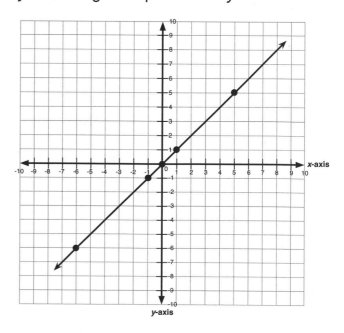

Chapter 3: Linear Equations and Inequalities (cont.)

3   Linear Inequalities in Two Variables

Like linear equations, the solution for linear inequalities is a set of numbers called an ordered pair that makes the inequality true or satisfies the inequality. An example of a linear inequality with two variables is $y > \frac{1}{2}x + 1$. When graphing inequalities, it is helpful to graph the associated equation of the inequality. An **associated equation** is the same sentence with an equal sign in place of the inequality sign. The associated equation for the inequality $y > \frac{1}{2}x + 1$ is $y = \frac{1}{2}x + 1$. In the graph below, a dotted line represents the associated equation. Since the inequality was >, the line is dotted indicating that the line is not included in the inequality. If the inequality was ≤ or ≥, this line would be a solid line because it is included in the inequality. Any number of ordered pairs above the line would be included in the solution set for the inequality $y > \frac{1}{2}x + 1$.

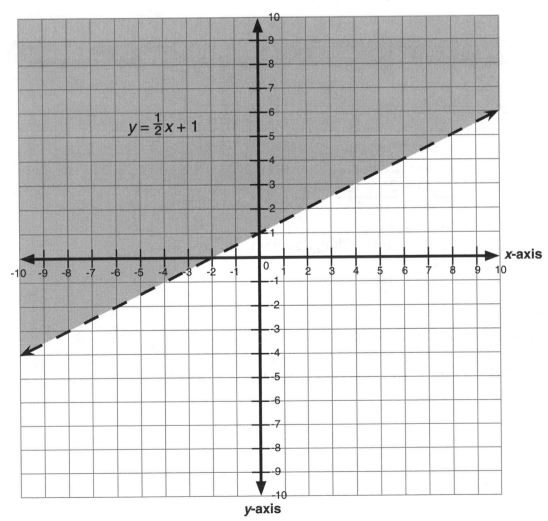

Chapter 3: Linear Equations and Inequalities (cont.)

④ Linear Systems

Equations with two variables have more than one solution. Using pairs of equations with the same variables, sometimes a solution can be found that makes both equations true. In the equations $x + y = 5$ and $x + 3 = y$, there is one value of x and one value for y (1, 4) that will make both statements true. Pairs of equations with the same two variables are called **systems of linear equations**. These equations can be solved by addition or subtraction, substitution, and graphing.

In solving systems of equations, identify the relationship between the two equations. Possible relationships include the coefficient of one of the x or y terms that is opposite the coefficient of the x or y term in the other equation. For example, $x + 3y = 7$ and $x - 3y = -2$. In this system, the y terms have opposite coefficients. The second kind of possible relationship is that the two equations have the same coefficient in front of one of the variables, such as $4x - y = 7$ and $4x + 2y = 10$. The coefficient in front of the two x variables is 4. Sometimes the coefficients of the two equations have no relationship to each other. An example of two equations with no relationship is $2x - 5y = 2$ and $-5x + 3y = 4$.

Example of Solving Systems if Equations Have Opposite Coefficients:

$3x - 2y = 5$ and $3x + 2y = 13$

Step 1: Add the equations.
$$3x - 2y = 5$$
$$\underline{+(3x + 2y = 13)}$$
$$6x \quad\quad = 18$$

Step 2: Solve the resulting equation.
$$6x = 18$$
$$\frac{6x}{6} = \frac{18}{6}$$

Answer: $x = 3$

Step 3: Substitute the answer back into one of the equations to solve for the other variable.
$$3x - 2y = 5$$
$$3(3) - 2y = 5$$
$$9 - 2y = 5$$
$$9 - 9 - 2y = 5 - 9$$
$$-2y = -4$$

Chapter 3: Linear Equations and Inequalities (cont.)

$$\frac{-2y}{-2} = \frac{-4}{-2}$$

Answer: $y = 2$

Step 4:   Check the answer.

$3x - 2y = 5$ $3x + 2y = 13$
$3(3) - 2(2) = 5$ $3(3) + 2(2) = 13$
$9 - 4 = 5$ $9 + 4 = 13$
$5 = 5$ $13 = 13$

Example of Solving Systems if Equations Have the Same Coefficients:

$4x - y = 7$ and $4x + 2y = 10$

Step 1:   Subtract the equations.

$$\begin{array}{r} 4x - y = 7 \\ -\,(4x + 2y = 10) \\ \hline -3y = -3 \end{array}$$

Step 2:   Solve the resulting equation.

$-3y = -3$

$$\frac{-3y}{-3} = \frac{-3}{-3}$$

Answer: $y = 1$

Step 3:   Substitute the answer back into one of the equations to solve for the other variable.

$4x - y = 7$
$4x - 1 = 7$
$4x - 1 + 1 = 7 + 1$
$4x = 8$

$$\frac{4x}{4} = \frac{8}{4}$$

Answer: $x = 2$

Step 4:   Check the answer.

$4x - y = 7$ $4x + 2y = 10$
$4(2) - 1 = 7$ $4(2) + 2(1) = 10$
$8 - 1 = 7$ $8 + 2 = 10$
$7 = 7$ $10 = 10$

Chapter 3: Linear Equations and Inequalities (cont.)

Example of Solving Systems if Equations Have No Relationship:

$2x - 5y = 2$ $\qquad\qquad$ $-5x + 3y = 4$

Step 1: Multiply the first equation by the coefficient in front of the x in the second equation.

$-5(2x - 5y = 2)$
$-5(2x) - -5(5y) = -5(2)$
$-10x + 25y = -10$

Step 2: Multiply the second equation by the coefficient in front of the x of the first equation.

$2(-5x + 3y = 4)$
$2(-5x) + 2(3y) = 2(4)$
$-10x + 6y = 8$

Step 3: Add or subtract these two new equations. Coefficients are the same, so subtract.

$$\begin{aligned}-10x + 25y &= -10 \\ -\ (-10x + 6y &= 8) \\ \hline 19y &= -18\end{aligned}$$

Step 4: Solve the resulting equation.

$19y = -18$

$\dfrac{19y}{19} = \dfrac{-18}{19}$

Answer: $y = -\dfrac{18}{19}$

Step 5: Substitute the answer back into one of the equations to solve for the other variable.

$2x - 5y = 2$

$2x - 5(-\tfrac{18}{19}) = 2$

$2x + \tfrac{90}{19} = 2$

$2x + \tfrac{90}{19} - \tfrac{90}{19} = 2 - \tfrac{90}{19}$

$2x = \tfrac{38}{19} - \tfrac{90}{19}$

$2x = -\tfrac{52}{19}$

$\dfrac{2x}{2} = (-\tfrac{52}{19}) \div 2$

Answer: $x = -\tfrac{26}{19}$

Chapter 3: Linear Equations and Inequalities (cont.)

Step 6: Check the answer.

$2x - 5y = 2$ $-5x + 3y = 4$

$2(-\frac{26}{19}) - 5(-\frac{18}{19}) = 2$ $-5(-\frac{26}{19}) + 3(-\frac{18}{19}) = 4$

$-\frac{52}{19} - (-\frac{90}{19}) = 2$ $\frac{130}{19} + -\frac{54}{19} = 4$

$\frac{38}{19} = 2$ $\frac{76}{19} = 4$

$2 = 2$ $4 = 4$

Example of Solving Linear Equations by Substitution:

$x - y = 3$ $2x + y = 12$

Step 1: Solve one of the equations for x.

$x - y = 3$

$x - y + y = 3 + y$

$x = 3 + y$

Step 2: Substitute the value for x in the other equation.

$2x + y = 12$

$2(3 + y) + y = 12$

Step 3: Solve the equation for y.

$6 + 2y + y = 12$

$6 + 3y = 12$

$6 - 6 + 3y = 12 - 6$

$3y = 6$

$\frac{3y}{3} = \frac{6}{3}$

Answer: $y = 2$

Step 4: Substitute the value of y into one of the original equations to find x.

$x - y = 3$

$x - 2 = 3$

$x - 2 + 2 = 3 + 2$

Answer: $x = 5$

Step 5: Check the answers in the original equations.

$x - y = 3$ $2x + y = 12$

$5 - 2 = 3$ $2(5) + 2 = 12$

$3 = 3$ $10 + 2 = 12$

                                     $12 = 12$

Name: _____ Date: _____

Chapter 3: Linear Equations and Inequalities (cont.)

Practice: Linear Equations and Inequalities

Solving Linear Equations With Two Variables
For questions 1–3, find the ordered pairs that make these statements true if *x* is {0, 1, 2, 3, 4}.
Work the problems on scratch paper.

1. $3x + 2y = 7$

x	y

Solution set:

_____

2. $y = 8x + 16$

x	y

Solution set:

_____

3. $y = 4x + 20$

x	y

Solution set:

_____

Graphing Linear Equations With Two Variables
Using the solution sets from problems 1–3, graph the equations.

4. $3x + 2y = 7$

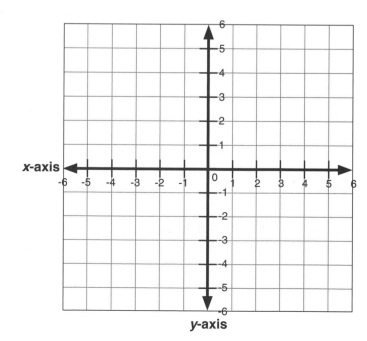

Name: _____ Date: _____

Chapter 3: Linear Equations and Inequalities (cont.)

Graph the solutions for 5–6 on the same graph. Be sure to label each line.

5. $y = 8x + 16$ **6.** $y = 4x + 20$

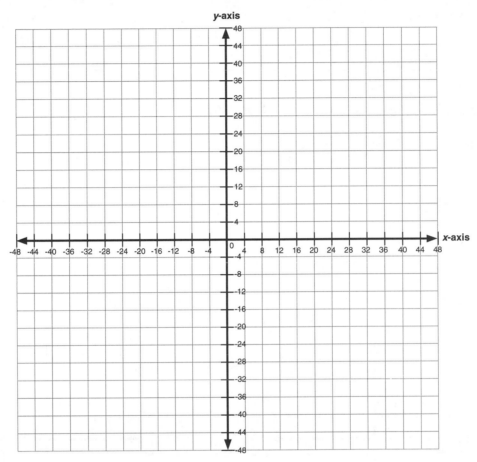

7. Using the graphs in problems 4–6, what would y be if $x = -2$?

   Problem A: $3x + 2y = 7$ If $x = -2$, then $y =$ _____

   Problem B: $y = 8x + 16$ If $x = -2$, then $y =$ _____

   Problem C: $y = 4x + 20$ If $x = -2$, then $y =$ _____

8. Using the formulas below, check your answers in number 7.

   Problem A: $3x + 2y = 7$ If $x = -2$

Name: _____   Date: _____

Chapter 3: Linear Equations and Inequalities (cont.)

Problem B: $y = 8x + 16$ If $x = -2$

Problem C: $y = 4x + 20$ If $x = -2$

For questions 9–10, graph the linear inequalities.

9. $3x + 2y + 4 \geq 0$

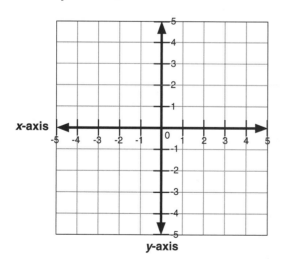

10. $5x - 4y > 10$

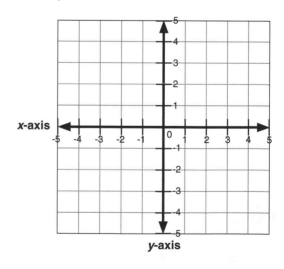

Solve the systems of equations for questions 11–14. Show your work on your own paper.

11. $x + 4y = 17$ and $-x - 2y = -9$

  $y =$ _____ $x =$ _____

12. $\frac{1}{4}x + 3y = 6$ and $\frac{1}{4}x + y = 4$

  $y =$ _____ $x =$ _____

13. $3x - 2y = 9$ and $-x + 3y = 4$

  $y =$ _____ $x =$ _____

14. $x - 3y = 0$ and $x + 3y = 6$

  $y =$ _____ $x =$ _____

50

Chapter 3: Linear Equations and Inequalities (cont.)

Summary of Linear Equations and Inequalities

A linear equation is any equation that can be put into the general form, $ax + by = c$ where a and b can be any real numbers. The Equal Addition Rule, Equal Subtraction Rule, Equal Multiplication Rule, and the Equal Division Rule help solve linear equations and inequalities.

Graphs or coordinate planes can be used to show number relationships of ordered pairs. The number line that measures distance from left to right (horizontally), moving from negative number values to positive number values, is called the **x-axis**. The number line that measures distance from bottom to top (vertically), moving from negative values to positive values, is called the **y-axis**. By breaking up the plane using these two axes, the plane is divided into four sections or quarters, called **quadrants**. Graphs can be used to represent and solve linear equations.

Equations with two variables have more than one solution. Pairs of equations with the same two variables are called systems of linear equations. These equations can be solved by addition or subtraction, substitution, and graphing.

Tips to Remember

Linear equations and inequalities can be solved following these steps:
- ☐ Simplify each side of the equation using the rules for the order of operation.
- ☐ Add and/or subtract the same number and/or variable from both sides of the equation.
- ☐ Multiply and/or divide both sides of the equation by the same number.
- ☐ Check your work using the answer.

Real Life Applications of Linear Equations and Inequalities

Linear equations can be used in studying the speed of different wildlife, population studies, page layout and design, temperature change, marine biology, framing pictures and finding costs, rates, averages, and percentages. Linear equations are also used in ecology, chemistry, retail sales, and purchasing.

Graphs are used to determine trends in shopping patterns, scores, and data collected in an investigation. Graphs are also used to make predictions. When determining whether or not an object can sink or float in water, a graph can be used. Density is the mass per unit volume. If data on the mass and volume of each object is collected for a set of objects, the mass and volume become points on the graph. These points can be plotted and compared to the density of water to determine whether the object will sink or float.

Chapter 4: Polynomial Products and Factors

Introduction to the Concepts of Polynomial Products and Factors

An expression is a certain number or variable, or numbers and variables, combined by operations such as addition, subtraction, multiplication, and/or division. There are monomial and polynomial algebraic expressions. Special kinds of polynomial expressions are binomial and trinomial expressions. This section examines the polynomial products and factors.

Concepts of Polynomial Products and Factors

1 Polynomials

2 Laws of Exponents

3 Multiplying Polynomials

4 Factoring Polynomials

5 Solving Polynomial Equations

6 Problem Solving Using Polynomial Equations

Explanations of the Concepts Related to Polynomial Products and Factors

1 **Polynomials**

Monomial expressions are of the form ax^n, where a is any real number, and the exponent n is a non-negative or positive integer or zero. 14, x, and $-6x^2y$ are monomial expressions. **Polynomial expressions** are a sum of monomial expressions. An example of a polynomial expression is $x^2 + (-4x) + (-5)$. Special kinds of polynomial expressions are binomial and trinomial expressions. **Binomials** are the sum of two monomials, for example $2x - 9$ or $2ab + b^2$. **Trinomial expressions** are the sum of three monomial terms, for example $x^3 - 5x - 3$ or $a^2 + 3ab - 5b^2$. This section examines the operations performed on algebraic expressions.

Remember that mathematics has four basic operations that can be performed: addition, subtraction, multiplication, and division. The operations listed are used to act on terms. A **term** can be a number (like 6), it can be a variable (like m), or it can be a product or quotient of numbers and variables (like $6m$ or $\frac{7m}{8}$). At times, we will need to know if terms can be called **like terms**. For example, $12xy$ and $-7xy$ are like terms because their variable parts are exactly alike. An example of terms that are unlike would be $12xy$ and $-7x^2y$. The variables used are the same (x's and y's), but in one term, the x is raised to the second power—this causes the

Chapter 4: Polynomial Products and Factors (cont.)

terms to be unlike. In a term that combines numbers and variables, like the monomial $4a$, the number 4 is called the **coefficient**. In the term $12xy$, the coefficient would be 12. Determining like terms and unlike terms and the meaning of the coefficient is important in being able to work with numbers, variables, and operations.

Examples of Monomial Expressions:

$$12 \qquad a \qquad \tfrac{1}{2}r \qquad -3xy$$

Notice that the monomial expressions above all include a number, variable, or the product of a number and one or more variables.

Examples of Binomial Expressions:

$$x + 3 \qquad\qquad x - 7$$

The binomial expressions above have two unlike terms combined by an addition or subtraction sign.

Examples of Trinomial Expressions:

$$x - y + 8 \qquad\qquad 2x - 6 + 4x$$

Notice the trinomial expressions above have three unlike terms combined by an addition or subtraction sign.

Examples of Polynomial Expressions:

$$z + a + b - a \qquad\qquad 2z + 4c + 2 - y$$

As shown in the examples above, polynomial expressions have one, two, three, or more terms combined by an addition or subtraction sign. A polynomial expression is the sum of the number, or variable, or the product of a number and one or more variables.

Chapter 4: Polynomial Products and Factors (cont.)

To simplify polynomials, regroup the expressions so that all the same degrees of the terms are together and do the operations the signs indicate.

Example of Simplifying Polynomial Expressions:

$x - 3x^2 + 6 + x^2 - 1 + 4x$

Step 1: Regroup the terms.

$(-3x^2 + x^2) + (x + 4x) + (6 - 1)$

Step 2: Do the operations indicated.

$-2x^2 + 5x + 5$

This polynomial is simplified, and the degree of the polynomial is 2.

To add two or more polynomials, write their sum and then simplify by combining the terms.

Example of Adding Polynomial Expressions:

$3x^2 + 6x - 5$ and $3x^3 + 2x^2 + 4x - 1$

Step 1: Add the like terms.

$(3x^2 + 6x - 5) + (3x^3 + 2x^2 + 4x - 1) = 3x^3 + 5x^2 + 10x - 6$

This can also be written like this:

$$3x^3 + 2x^2 + 4x - 1$$
$$+ \quad\quad 3x^2 + 6x - 5$$
$$\overline{3x^3 + 5x^2 + 10x - 6}$$

To subtract two or more polynomials, write their difference and then simplify by combining the terms.

Example of Subtracting Polynomial Expressions:

$3x^2 + 6x - 5$ from $3x^3 + 2x^2 + 4x - 1$

Step 1: Subtract the like terms.

$(3x^3 + 2x^2 + 4x - 1) - (3x^2 + 6x - 5) = 3x^3 - x^2 + 2x - 4$

This can also be written like this:

$$3x^3 + 2x^2 + 4x - 1$$
$$- \quad\quad 3x^2 + 6x - 5$$
$$\overline{3x^3 \ - x^2 + 2x - 4}$$

Chapter 4: Polynomial Products and Factors (cont.)

❷ Laws of Exponents

Using the Laws of Exponents will help when multiplying polynomials. The Laws of Exponents include: If a and b are real numbers and n and m are positive integers, then $a^m \cdot a^n = a^{m+n}$, $(ab)^m = a^m b^m$, $(a^m)^n = a^{mn}$.

Example of The First Law of Exponents, $a^m \cdot a^n = a^{m+n}$:

$$x^2 \cdot x^3 = x^{2+3} = x^5$$

Example of the Second Law of Exponents, $(ab)^m = a^m b^m$:

$$(xy)^2 = x^2 y^2$$

Example of the Third Law of Exponents $(a^m)^n = a^{mn}$:

$$(c^2)^3 = c^{2(3)} = c^6$$

❸ Multiplying Polynomials

When you have both the operation of addition and the operation of multiplication to do, you can decide which you want to do first. Suppose you have $3(2 + 5)$ to simplify. Notice that you have addition in the parentheses and then you need to multiply by 3. So by order of operations, $3(2 + 5) = 3(7) = 21$. But we could do the multiplication first, as long as we distribute. What does this mean? Think about an arrow that links 3 to each part of the addition problem.

$$3(2 + 5) = 3 \cdot 2 + 3 \cdot 5 = 6 + 15 = 21$$

Notice that this answer, when we distribute, multiply first, and then add, is the same as our first answer. In general, $a(b + c) = a \cdot b + a \cdot c$ for any real numbers. This property is usually called the **Distributive Property**.

Examples Using the Distributive Property:

$$3(x + 7) = 3 \cdot x + 3 \cdot 7 = 3x + 21$$

$$b(b + 1) = b \cdot b + b \cdot 1 = b^2 + b$$

Chapter 4: Polynomial Products and Factors (cont.)

To multiply polynomials, use the distributive property. First multiply each term of one polynomial by each term of the other polynomial, and then add the resulting monomials.

Example of Multiplying Polynomials:

Step 1: $(3x + 2)(x^2 + 2x - 3)$
Multiply each term of one by each term of the other.
$3x(x^2 + 2x - 3) + 2(x^2 + 2x - 3)$
$(3x^3 + 6x^2 - 9x) + (2x^2 + 4x - 6)$

Step 2: Add the expressions together.

$$
\begin{array}{r}
3x^3 + 6x^2 - 9x \\
+ \qquad 2x^2 + 4x - 6 \\
\hline
3x^3 + 8x^2 - 5x - 6
\end{array}
$$

When multiplying polynomials, it is helpful to memorize certain special products. **Special products** are products that occur frequently. Special products include the following:

$(a + b)^2 = a^2 + 2ab + b^2$	Perfect Square Trinomial
$(a - b)^2 = a^2 - 2ab + b^2$	Perfect Square Trinomial
$(a + b)(a - b) = a^2 - b^2$	Difference of Squares
$a^3 + b^3 = (a + b)(a^2 - ab + b^2)$	Sum of Cubes
$a^3 - b^3 = (a - b)(a^2 + ab + b^2)$	Difference of Cubes

4   Factoring Polynomials

Polynomials can be factored by using the **greatest common factor** (**GCF**), recognizing special products, and by grouping terms. The first step to factoring polynomials is to find the GCF.

Example of Factoring Polynomials GCF:

Step 1: $2x^4 - 4x^3 + 8x^2$
Find the GCF of $2x^4 - 4x^3 + 8x^2$ GCF $= 2x^2$
Factor out the GCF. $2x^2(x^2 - 2x + 4)$

The factors of this polynomial are $2x^2$ and $x^2 - 2x + 4$.

Chapter 4: Polynomial Products and Factors (cont.)

Sometimes you need more than one step to factor polynomials, but the first step is always to look for and factor out the GCF.

Examples of Factoring Polynomials With More Than One Step:

Step 1: $3z^5 - 48z$
GCF $= 3z$

Step 2: Factor out the GCF. $3z(z^4 - 16)$
$3z[(z^2)^2 - (4)^2]$ Difference of Squares
$3z(z^2 + 4)(z^2 - 4)$ $4 = 2^2$
$3z(z^2 + 4)(z + 2)(z - 2)$ Difference of Squares again

Step 1: $a^3 - 1$
GCF $= a - 1$

Step 2: Factor out the GCF. $(a - 1)(a^2 + a + 1)$ Difference of Cubes

❺ Solving Polynomial Equations

Factoring can be used to solve polynomial equations. A **polynomial equation** has a polynomial on one side of the equation and zero on the other side of the equation. A **root** or **solution** of a polynomial equation is a value that satisfies the equation or makes it true. The **zero product property** states $ab = 0$ if $a = 0$ or $b = 0$. To use the zero product property to solve a polynomial equation, write the equation with 0 on one side, and factor the other side of the equation. Solve the equation by writing each factor into an equation that is equal to 0.

Example of Solving an Equation Using the Zero Product Property:

Step 1: $x^2 - 3x - 10$
Write the equation = to 0.
$x^2 - 3x - 10 = 0$

Step 2: Factor the other side.
$(x - 5)(x + 2) = 0$

Step 3: Write each factor as an equation that is equal to 0.
$(x - 5) = 0$ $(x + 2) = 0$

Step 4: Solve the equations.
$x - 5 = 0$ $x + 2 = 0$
$x - 5 + 5 = 0 + 5$ $x + 2 - 2 = 0 - 2$
$x = 5$ $x = \text{-}2$

Chapter 4: Polynomial Products and Factors (cont.)

Step 5: Check the answers in the original equation.

$x^2 - 3x - 10 = 0$	$x^2 - 3x - 10 = 0$
$5^2 - 3(5) - 10 = 0$	$-2^2 - 3(-2) - 10 = 0$
$25 - 15 - 10 = 0$	$4 + 6 - 10 = 0$
$10 - 10 = 0$	$10 - 10 = 0$
$0 = 0$	$0 = 0$

Answer: Solution set is $\{5, -2\}$

⓺ Problem Solving Using Polynomial Equations

Solving polynomial equations can be used to solve mathematical models. A **mathematical model** is an equation that represents a real-life problem.

Example of Using a Polynomial Equation to Solve a Mathematical Model:

Problem: An artist is matting a painting. The area of the mat and painting is 680 in.^{2} The painting is twice as long as it is wide. The mat border is 3 inches wide. What are the dimensions of the painting itself?

Area is equal to the length multiplied by the width. $A = l(w) = 680$ in.^{2}
The length is twice as long as the width.
Let the length be represented by $2w$.
Let the width be represented by w.
Because the mat has a three-inch border around all sides, the dimension of the mat is 6 inches larger than the painting.

Step 1: Write the equation. $l(w) = A$
$(2w + 6)(w + 6) = 680$ in.^{2}

Step 2: Simplify.
$(2w + 6)(w + 6) = 680$

$$\frac{2(w + 3)(w + 6)}{2} = \frac{680}{2}$$

$(w + 3)(w + 6) = 340$
$w^2 + 9w + 18 = 340$

Step 3: Write the equation = to 0.
$w^2 + 9w + 18 = 340$

Chapter 4: Polynomial Products and Factors (cont.)

$w^2 + 9w + 18 - 340 = 340 - 340$
$w^2 + 9w - 322 = 0$

Step 4:   Factor the other side.
$(w - 14)(w + 23) = 0$

Step 5:   Write each factor as an equation that is equal to 0.
$w - 14 = 0$ $w + 23 = 0$

Step 6:   Solve the equations.

$w - 14 = 0$ $w + 23 = 0$
$w - 14 + 14 = 0 + 14$ $w + 23 - 23 = 0 - 23$
$w = 14$ $w = -23$
                                         Reject—cannot have a negative
                                         width measurement.

Answer: The print's width is 14 inches, and the length is twice as long, or 28 inches.

Step 7:   Check the answers in the original equation.
$(2w + 6)(w + 6) = 680$ in.^{2}
$(28 + 6)(14 + 6) = 680$
$(28 + 6)(20) = 680$
$(34)(20) = 680$
$680 = 680$

The solution: The painting is 28 inches long by 14 inches wide.

Name: _____ Date: _____

Chapter 4: Polynomial Products and Factors (cont.)

Practice: Polynomial Products and Factors

Simplify the polynomials.

1. $2x - 5x^2 + 3 + x^2 - 1 + 2x$

_____

2. $4x - 3x^3 + 6 + x^2 + 1x^3 + 1x$

_____

Add the polynomials. Show your work on your own paper.

3. $7x^2 + 2x + 5$ and $3x^3 + 2x^2 + 4x - 1$

_____

4. $x^2 + 6x + 5$ and $3x^3 + 2x^2 + 4x - 1$

_____

Subtract the polynomials. Show your work on your own paper.

5. $3 + 2x^3 + 2x + 3$ from $3x^3 + 2x^2 + 4x - 1$ _____

6. $2x^2 + 6x - 3x^3$ from $3x^3 + 2x^2 + 4x - 1$ _____

Laws of Exponents
Using the Laws of Exponents, simplify problems 7–12, assuming that the variable exponents are positive integers. Identify which law the problem represents.

7. $3a^3 \cdot 4a^4$ _____ _____

8. $(2c^2d^3)^3$ _____ _____

9. $(xy)^3$ _____ _____

10. $3x^2 \cdot 2x^4$ _____ _____

11. $(4b^2c)^3$ _____ _____

12. $(yz)^5$ _____ _____

Multiplying Polynomials
For questions 13–16, multiply each of the polynomials using the distributive property. Show your work on your own paper.

13. $(3x + 1)(2x - 7)$

_____

14. $(5a - 9)(3a + 2)$

_____

Name: _____   Date: _____

Chapter 4: Polynomial Products and Factors (cont.)

15. $(2y - 3)^2$

_____

16. $(x^2 + 2x + 3)(2x^2 - 2x + 2)$

_____

Factoring Polynomials

Factor the polynomials in questions 17–20. Show your work on your own paper.

17. $a^2 + 6a + 9$

_____

18. $25x^2 - 16a^2$

_____

19. $8x^3 + y^3$

_____

20. $9x^2 - 12x + 4$

_____

Solving Polynomial Equations

Solve the following polynomial equations. Show your work on your own paper.

21. $y^2 = y + 12$

Solution set = _____

22. $x^2 = x + 30$

Solution set = _____

Problem Solving Using Polynomial Equations

23. A rocket is shot straight up at the speed of 96 ft./sec. How long is the rocket in the air before it lands? Vertical motion is only affected by gravity. The gravitational constant is 32 ft./sec². To determine the height, use the formula $h = vt - 16t^2$. Use v to represent velocity, h for the height, and t for the number of seconds. Show your work on your own paper.

_____

Chapter 4: Polynomial Products and Factors (cont.)

Summary of Polynomial Products and Factors

- Polynomial expressions have one, two, three, or more terms combined by an addition or subtraction sign. To simplify polynomials, regroup the expressions so that all the same degrees of the terms are together and do the operations the signs indicate.

- The Laws of Exponents are: If a and b are real numbers and n and m are positive integers, then $a^m \cdot a^n = a^{m+n}$, $(ab)^m = a^m b^m$, $(a^m)^n = a^{mn}$.

- The Distributive Property states that $a(b + c) = a \cdot b + a \cdot c$ for any real numbers. To multiply polynomials, use the Distributive Property. First multiply each term of one polynomial by each term of the other polynomial, and then add the resulting monomials.

- Special products are products that occur frequently. Memorize the special products. For example:

$(a + b)^2 = a^2 + 2ab + b^2$	Perfect Square Trinomial
$(a - b)^2 = a^2 - 2ab + b^2$	Perfect Square Trinomial
$(a + b)(a - b) = a^2 - b^2$	Difference of Squares
$a^3 + b^3 = (a + b)(a^2 - ab + b^2)$	Sum of Cubes
$a^3 - b^3 = (a - b)(a^2 + ab + b^2)$	Difference of Cubes

- Polynomials can be factored by using the greatest common factor (GCF), recognizing special products, and by grouping terms.

- A polynomial equation has a polynomial on one side of the equation and zero on the other side of the equation. A root or solution of a polynomial equation is a value that satisfies the equation or makes it true. The zero product property states that $ab = 0$ if $a = 0$ or $b = 0$.
    To use the zero product property to solve a polynomial equation:
    1. Write the equation = to 0.   2. Factor the other side.
    3. Write each factor as an equation that is equal to 0.
    4. Solve the equations.   5. Check the answers in the original equation.

Tips to Remember

- When adding or subtracting polynomials, make sure you match up all of the terms that are alike.

- Use the FOIL process when multiplying polynomials. FOIL stands for **F**irst terms, **O**utside terms, **I**nside terms, **L**ast terms.

Real Life Applications of Polynomial Products and Factors

Artists can use polynomial equations to frame and mat pictures. Farmers can use polynomial equations to determine the amount of fencing needed or the amount of seeds to buy to plant a field.

Chapter 5: Rational Algebraic Expressions

Introduction to Rational Algebraic Expressions

A rational number can be expressed as a quotient of integers. A rational expression can be expressed as a quotient of polynomials. This section reviews the Laws of Exponents and rational algebraic expressions.

Concepts of Rational Algebraic Expressions

① Review of the Laws of Exponents

② Rational Algebraic Expressions

③ Problem Solving Using Fractional Expressions

Explanations of Concepts of Rational Algebraic Expressions

① **Review of the Laws of Exponents**

The Laws of Exponents include: If n and m are positive integers and a and b are real numbers, with $a \neq 0$ and $b \neq 0$ when they are divisors, then: $a^m \cdot a^n = a^{m+n}$; $(ab)^m = a^m b^m$; $(a^m)^n = a^{mn}$; if $m > n$, $\dfrac{a^m}{a^n} = a^{m-n}$; if $n > m$, $\dfrac{a^m}{a^n} = \dfrac{1}{a^{n-m}}$; and $\left(\dfrac{a}{b}\right)^m = \dfrac{a^m}{b^m}$.

Examples of the First Law of Exponents, $a^m \cdot a^n = a^{m+n}$:

$$x^2 \cdot x^3 = x^{2+3} = x^5 \qquad\qquad 3^5 \cdot 3^7 = 3^{5+7} = 3^{12}$$

Examples of the Second Law of Exponents, $(ab)^m = a^m b^m$:

$$(xy)^2 = x^2 y^2 \qquad\qquad (4 \cdot 5)^2 = 4^2 \cdot 5^2$$

Examples of the Third Law of Exponents, $(a^m)^n = a^{mn}$:

$$(c^2)^3 = c^{2(3)} = c^6 \qquad\qquad (5^2)^3 = 5^{2(3)} = 5^6$$

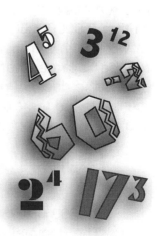

Chapter 5: Rational Algebraic Expressions (cont.)

Examples of the Fourth Law of Exponents:

If $m > n$, $\dfrac{a^m}{a^n} = a^{m-n}$ $\qquad\qquad$ If $n > m$, $\dfrac{a^m}{a^n} = \dfrac{1}{a^{n-m}}$

If $m > n$, $\dfrac{2^5}{2^2} = 2^{5-2} = 2^3$ $\qquad\qquad$ If $n > m$, $\dfrac{5^2}{5^4} = \dfrac{1}{5^{4-2}} = \dfrac{1}{5^2}$

If $m > n$, $\dfrac{x^5}{x^3} = x^{5-3} = x^2$ $\qquad\qquad$ If $n > m$, $\dfrac{y^2}{y^5} = \dfrac{1}{y^{5-2}} = \dfrac{1}{y^3}$

If $m > n$, $\dfrac{3^5}{3^3} = 3^{5-3} = 3^2$ $\qquad\qquad$ If $n > m$, $\dfrac{3^2}{3^5} = \dfrac{1}{3^{5-2}} = \dfrac{1}{3^3}$

Example of the Fifth Law of Exponents:

$\left(\dfrac{a}{b}\right)^m = \dfrac{a^m}{b^m}$ $\qquad\qquad$ $\left(\dfrac{3}{4}\right)^2 = \dfrac{3^2}{4^2}$

When expressions have exponents of zero or a negative number, follow the laws of exponents. If n is a positive integer and $a \neq 0$: $a^0 = 1$ and $a^{-n} = \dfrac{1}{a^n}$. The expression 0^0 is not defined.

Scientists use exponents for scientific notation to express very large or very small numbers. Light travels a distance of 5,680,000,000,000 miles in a year. In scientific notation, a number is expressed as $m \times 10^n$. The distance light travels could be expressed as 5.68×10^{12}. A neutron has a mass of 1.675×10^{-27}. Without scientific notation, the mass of a neutron would be written 0.000000000000000000000000001675. Using scientific notation helps make it easier to work with numbers like these. When writing a given number in scientific notation, if the number is larger than one, the decimal is moved to the left. The exponent identifies how many places the decimal point was moved. If the number is less than one, the decimal is moved to the right, and the exponent shows the number of places the decimal moved, but the exponent is a negative number.

Examples of Changing Numbers into Scientific Notation:

$89{,}363 = 8.9363 \times 10^4$
The decimal was moved 4 places to the left, and the number is greater than 1, so the decimal moves left.
$0.000000883 = 8.83 \times 10^{-7}$

Chapter 5: Rational Algebraic Expressions (cont.)

The number is less than 1, so the decimal is moved to the left, and the exponent is negative.

When reversing the process and changing from scientific notation to numbers, if the exponent is negative, move the decimal to the left the number of places equal to the exponent. If the exponent is positive, move the decimal to the right.

Examples of Changing Scientific Notation Into Numbers:

$7.345 \times 10^{-4} = 0.0007345$
Negative exponent, move decimal left.

$6.77 \times 10^{5} = 677,000$
Positive exponent, move decimal right.

$$0.000000000000000000000000001675 = 1.675 \times 10^{-27}$$

2 Rational Algebraic Expressions

A rational number can be expressed as a quotient of integers. A rational expression can be expressed as a quotient of polynomials. A rational expression is in its simplest form when the quotient of the polynomials have a greatest common factor (GCF) of 1. Examples of rational expressions are $\dfrac{4x^2y}{3x}$, $\dfrac{x^2 - 3x - 4}{x^2 - 1}$, and $x(x^2 - 4)^{-1} = \dfrac{x}{x^2 - 4}$.

Example of Simplifying Rational Expressions:

$$\frac{x^2 - 2x}{x^2 - 4} = \frac{x(x - 2)}{(x + 2)(x - 2)} = \frac{x(\cancel{x - 2})}{(x + 2)(\cancel{x - 2})} = \frac{x}{x + 2}$$

To multiply rational expressions, use the multiplication rule for multiplying fractions. The multiplication rule for fractions states that $\dfrac{a}{b} \cdot \dfrac{c}{d} = \dfrac{ac}{bd}$. Products of rational expressions should be expressed in simplest form.

Chapter 5: Rational Algebraic Expressions (cont.)

Example of Multiplying Rational Expressions:

$$\frac{3x^2 - 6x}{x^2 - 6x + 9} \cdot \frac{x^2 - x - 6}{x^2 - 4}$$

Step 1:   Factor both expressions.
$$\frac{3x^2 - 6x}{x^2 - 6x + 9} \cdot \frac{x^2 - x - 6}{x^2 - 4}$$

$$\frac{3x(x-2)}{(x-3)(x-3)} \cdot \frac{(x+2)(x-3)}{(x+2)(x-2)}$$

$$\frac{3x(x-2)}{(x-3)(x-3)} \cdot \frac{(\cancel{x+2})(x-3)}{(\cancel{x+2})(x-2)}$$

$$\frac{3x(x-2)}{(x-3)(x-3)} \cdot \frac{(x-3)}{(x-2)}$$

Step 2:   Multiply the expressions.
$$\frac{3x(x-2)(x-3)}{(x-3)(x-3)(x-2)}$$

$$\frac{3x(\cancel{x-2})(\cancel{x-3})}{(x-3)(\cancel{x-3})(\cancel{x-2})}$$

$$\frac{3x}{x-3}$$

For every real number a and nonzero real number b, the definition of division is the quotient a divided by b and is written as $\frac{a}{b}$ or $a \div b$. For every real number a and nonzero real number b, $\frac{a}{b} = a \cdot \frac{1}{b}$ or $a \div b = a \cdot \frac{1}{b}$ as long as $b \neq 0$. Zero is not used because 0 has no reciprocal. Division by 0 is not defined. Rules for division state that the quotient of two positive or two negative numbers is a positive number, and the quotient of one positive and one negative number is negative.

Chapter 5: Rational Algebraic Expressions (cont.)

Examples of Division of Rational Expressions:

$$\frac{14}{15} \div \frac{7}{5}$$

Step 1: Dividing is the same as multiplying by the reciprocal.

$$\frac{14}{15} \cdot \frac{5}{7}$$

Step 2: $\dfrac{2(7) \cdot 5}{3(5) \cdot 7}$ = Dividing the common factors.

Answer: $\dfrac{2}{3}$

$$\frac{6xy}{a^2} \div \frac{3y}{a^3x}$$

Step 1: Dividing is the same as multiplying by the reciprocal.

$$\frac{6xy}{a^2} \cdot \frac{a^3x}{3y}$$

Step 2: Divide by common factors y, 3, a^2.

Answer: $2ax^2$

Example of a Division Problem—Writing Out the Problem With a Division Sign:

$$\frac{\dfrac{a^2 - 4ab + 3b^2}{a + 2b}}{a^2 - ab - 6b^2}$$

Step 1: Write out the problem first with a division sign.

$$\frac{a^2 - 4ab + 3b^2}{a + 2b} \div \frac{a^2 - ab - 6b^2}{1}$$

Step 2: Change the divisor to its reciprocal.

$$\frac{a^2 - 4ab + 3b^2}{a + 2b} \cdot \frac{1}{a^2 - ab - 6b^2}$$

Chapter 5: Rational Algebraic Expressions (cont.)

Step 3:   Factor.

$$\frac{(a-b)(a-3b)}{a+2b} \cdot \frac{1}{(a+2b)(a-3b)}$$

Step 4:   Divide by the common factor $(a-3b)$.

$$\frac{(a-b)\cancel{(a-3b)}}{a+2b} \cdot \frac{1}{(a+2b)\cancel{(a-3b)}}$$

Step 5:   Multiply.

$$\frac{a-b}{a+2b} \cdot \frac{1}{a+2b} = \frac{a-b}{(a+2b)^2}$$

There are two rules for adding and subtracting fractions with equal denominators. These two rules can be used with more than two terms. These two rules state:

$$\frac{a}{c} + \frac{b}{c} = \frac{a+b}{c}$$

$$\frac{a}{c} - \frac{b}{c} = \frac{a-b}{c}$$

Examples of Adding and Subtracting Fractions With Equal Denominators:

Add: $\dfrac{2}{5} + \dfrac{4}{5}$

Step 1:   Add the numerators and put them over the same denominator.

$$\frac{2}{5} + \frac{4}{5} = \frac{2+4}{5} = \frac{6}{5}$$

Subtract: $\dfrac{3}{4} - \dfrac{1}{4}$

Step 1:   Subtract the numerators and put them over the same denominator.

$$\frac{3}{4} - \frac{1}{4} = \frac{3-1}{4} = \frac{2}{4} = \frac{1}{2}$$

Chapter 5: Rational Algebraic Expressions (cont.)

When adding or subtracting fractions with different denominators, use these rules. Find the least common denominator (LCD) or find the lowest common multiple of all of the denominators. Express each fraction with the equivalent factor with the LCD as the denominator. To do this, you need to multiply the numerator by the same number you multiply the denominator by to get the LCD. Then add or subtract the result.

Examples of Adding or Subtracting Fractions With Different Denominators:

Add: $\dfrac{23}{36} + \dfrac{4}{6}$

Step 1: The LCD = 36

Step 2: Find the factors that change 6 to 36. $6 \quad 6 = 36$

Step 3: Multiply the numerator by the same number as the denominator. In this case 6.
$$\frac{23}{36} + \frac{4(6)}{6(6)} = \frac{23}{36} + \frac{24}{36}$$

Step 4: Add or subtract the numbers. Since the denominators are the same, the first two rules apply.
$$\frac{23}{36} + \frac{24}{36} = \frac{23+24}{36} = \frac{47}{36}$$

Subtract: $\dfrac{1}{6a^2} - \dfrac{1}{2ab}$

Step 1: The LCD = $6a^2b$

Step 2: Find the factors that change both denominators to $6a^2b$. $6a^2(b) = 6a^2b$ and $2ab(3a) = 6a^2b$.

Step 3: Multiply the numerator by the same number as the denominator. In this case b and $3a$.
$$\frac{1}{6a^2} - \frac{1}{2ab} = \frac{1(b)}{6a^2(b)} - \frac{1(3a)}{2ab(3a)} = \frac{b}{6a^2b} - \frac{3a}{6a^2b}$$

Step 4: Add or subtract the numbers. Since the denominators are the same, the first two rules apply.
$$\frac{b}{6a^2b} - \frac{3a}{6a^2b} = \frac{b-3a}{6a^2b}$$

Chapter 5: Rational Algebraic Expressions (cont.)

When working with two or more polynomials, the LCM is the multiple having the least degree and least positive factor. When adding or subtracting fractions with trinomials, factor the denominators.

Example of Adding or Subtracting Fractions With Trinomial Denominators:

$$\frac{3}{x^2 + x - 6} - \frac{2}{x^2 - 3x + 2}$$

Step 1: Factor the denominators.

$$\frac{3}{x^2 + x - 6} - \frac{2}{x^2 - 3x + 2}$$

$$\frac{3}{(x-2)(x+3)} - \frac{2}{(x-1)(x-2)}$$

Step 2: The LCD $= (x-2)(x-1)(x+3)$

Step 3: Multiply the numerator by the same number as the denominator, in this case $(x-1)$ and $(x+3)$.

$$\frac{3(x-1)}{(x-2)(x+3)(x-1)} - \frac{2(x+3)}{(x-1)(x-2)(x+3)}$$

Step 4: Add or subtract the numbers. Since the denominators are the same, the first two rules apply.

$$\frac{3(x-1)}{(x-2)(x+3)(x-1)} - \frac{2(x+3)}{(x-1)(x-2)(x+3)} =$$

$$\frac{3x-3}{(x-2)(x+3)(x-1)} - \frac{2x+6}{(x-1)(x-2)(x+3)} =$$

$$\frac{3x-3-(2x+6)}{(x-2)(x+3)(x-1)} = \frac{3x-2x-3-6}{(x-1)(x-2)(x+3)} =$$

$$\frac{x-9}{(x-2)(x+3)(x-1)}$$

Chapter 5: Rational Algebraic Expressions (cont.)

③ Problem Solving Using Fractional Equations and Inequalities

To solve fractional equations and inequalities, multiply both sides of the open sentence by the LCD of the fractions. Then solve the equation or inequality as you would any other equation or inequality.

Example of Solving Fractional Equations:

$$\frac{c^2}{2} = \frac{2c}{15} + \frac{1}{10}$$

Step 1: The LCD = 30

Step 2: Multiply both sides by the LCD.
$$30\left(\frac{c^2}{2}\right) = 30\left(\frac{2c}{15} + \frac{1}{10}\right)$$

Step 3: Reduce the fractions.
$$\frac{30c^2}{2} = \frac{60c}{15} + \frac{30}{10}$$
$$15c^2 = 4c + 3$$

Step 4: Solve the equation by making it = 0.
$$15c^2 = 4c + 3$$
$$15c^2 - 4c - 3 = 4c + 3 - 4c - 3$$
$$15c^2 - 4c - 3 = 0$$

Step 5: Factor the left side.
$$(3c + 1)(5c - 3) = 0$$

Step 6: Set each factor = 0.
$$3c + 1 = 0 \qquad\qquad 5c - 3 = 0$$

Step 7: Solve.

$$3c + 1 - 1 = 0 - 1 \qquad\qquad 5c - 3 + 3 = 0 + 3$$
$$3c = -1 \qquad\qquad\qquad\qquad 5c = 3$$
$$\frac{3c}{3} = \frac{-1}{3} \qquad\qquad\qquad \frac{5c}{5} = \frac{3}{5}$$
$$c = -\frac{1}{3} \qquad\qquad\qquad\qquad c = \frac{3}{5}$$

Answer: The solution set is $\{-\frac{1}{3}, \frac{3}{5}\}$

Chapter 5: Rational Algebraic Expressions (cont.)

Example of Solving Fractional Inequalities:

$$\frac{a}{8} - \frac{a-2}{3} \geq \frac{a+1}{6} - 1$$

Step 1:   The LCD = 24

Step 2:   Multiply both sides by the LCD.

$$24\left(\frac{a}{8} - \frac{a-2}{3}\right) \geq 24\left(\frac{a+1}{6} - 1\right)$$

Step 3:   Reduce the fractions.

$$\frac{24a}{8} - \frac{24a-48}{3} \geq \frac{24a+24}{6} - 24$$

$$3a - 8a + 16 \geq 4a + 4 - 24$$

Step 4:   Solve the inequality.

$$-5a + 16 \geq 4a - 20$$

$$-5a + 16 - 4a - 16 \geq 4a - 20 - 4a - 16$$

$$-9a \geq -36$$

$$\frac{-9a}{-9} \leq \frac{-36}{-9}$$ Remember that when you divide by a negative number, reverse the inequality sign.

Answer: $a \leq 4$

Name: _____ Date: _____

Chapter 5: Rational Algebraic Expressions (cont.)

Practice: Rational Expressions

Laws of Exponents
Applying the laws of exponents, simplify the following expressions and show your work. Assume that no denominator equals 0.

1. $\dfrac{3^7}{3^4}$ _____

2. $\dfrac{3x^2}{x^6}$ _____

3. $\left(\dfrac{t^2}{3}\right)^3$ _____

4. $\dfrac{24x^3}{4x}$ _____

Using Scientific Notation
Write each number in scientific notation.

5. 0.000000789 _____

6. 186,000 _____

Write each scientific notation out in decimal form.

7. 6.75 10^4 _____

8. 7.50 10^{-10} _____

Multiplying and Dividing Rational Expressions
Show your work as you multiply or divide the rational expressions below.

9. $\dfrac{5x^3}{-3} \cdot \dfrac{-6}{10x^2}$

_____

10. $\dfrac{x^2}{4} \cdot \left(\dfrac{xy}{6}\right)^{-1} \cdot \dfrac{2y^2}{x}$

_____

11. $\dfrac{8a^2}{3} \div \dfrac{2a}{9}$

_____

12. $\dfrac{x^2-4}{2x^2-5x+2} \div \dfrac{2x^2-3x-2}{4x^2-1}$

_____

Name: _____ Date: _____

Chapter 5: Rational Algebraic Expressions (cont.)

Adding and Subtracting Rational Expressions

Show your work as you add or subtract the rational expressions below.

13. $\dfrac{3}{15} - \dfrac{10}{15} + \dfrac{5}{15}$

_____

14. $\dfrac{x+2}{12} + \dfrac{x-2}{6}$

_____

15. $\dfrac{1}{x^2 - 1} - \dfrac{1}{(x-1)^2}$

_____

16. $\dfrac{3}{a^2 - 5a + 6} + \dfrac{2}{a^2 - 4}$

_____

Solving Fractional Equations and Inequalities

On your own paper, show your work as you solve these fractional equations and inequalities.

17. $\dfrac{x^2}{3} - \dfrac{x}{6} = 1$

Solution set: _____

18. $\dfrac{x(x+1)}{5} - \dfrac{x+1}{6} = \dfrac{1}{3}$

Solution set: _____

19. $\dfrac{y^2 + 4}{6} + \dfrac{y+1}{3} < \dfrac{3}{2}$

Solution set: _____

20. Fred and Frank were looking at the length of a side of a square. Fred subtracted 1 from the length, squared the result, and then divided by 3. Frank added 2 to the number and then divided by 2. When they compared their answers, they found they now had the same number. What was the length of the side of the original square?

_____

Chapter 5: Rational Algebraic Expressions (cont.)

Summary of Rational Expressions

A rational number can be expressed as a quotient of integers or fractions. A rational expression can be expressed as a quotient of polynomials or fractions.

The Laws of Exponents include: If n and m are positive integers and a and b are real numbers, with $a \neq 0$ and $b \neq 0$ when they are divisors, then: $a^m \cdot a^n = a^{m+n}$, $(ab)^m = a^m b^m$, $(a^m)^n = a^{mn}$, If $m > n$, $\frac{a^m}{a^n} = a^{m-n}$, If $n > m$, $\frac{a^m}{a^n} = \frac{1}{a^{n-m}}$, and $(\frac{a}{b})^m = \frac{a^m}{b^m}$. When expressions have exponents of zero or a negative number, follow the laws of exponents. If n is a positive integer and $a \neq 0$: $a^0 = 1$ and $a^{-n} = \frac{1}{a^n}$. The expression 0^0 is not defined.

To multiply rational expressions, use the multiplication rule for multiplying fractions. The multiplication rule for fractions states that $\frac{a}{b} \cdot \frac{c}{d} = \frac{ac}{bd}$. Products of rational expressions should be expressed in simplest form.

For every real number a and nonzero real number b, the definition of division is the quotient a divided by b is written as $\frac{a}{b}$ or $a \div b$. For every real number a and nonzero real number b, $\frac{a}{b} = a \cdot \frac{1}{b}$ or $a \div b = a \cdot \frac{1}{b}$.

There are two rules for adding and subtracting fractions with equal denominators. These two rules can be used with more than two terms. These two rules state:

$$\frac{a}{c} + \frac{b}{c} = \frac{a+b}{c}$$

$$\frac{a}{c} - \frac{b}{c} = \frac{a-b}{c}$$

When adding or subtracting fractions with different denominators, use these rules. Find the least common denominator (LCD) or find the lowest common multiple of all of the denominators. Express each fraction with the equivalent factor with the LCD as the denominator.

When working with two or more polynomials, the LCM is the multiple having the least degree and least positive factor. When adding or subtracting fractions with trinomials, factor the denominators.

To solve equations and inequalities, multiply both sides of the open sentence by the LCD of the fractions. Then solve the equation or inequality as you would any other equation or inequality.

Chapter 5: Rational Algebraic Expressions (cont.)

Tips to Remember

When working with rational expressions, use the rules of exponents. A quick inspection can help you make sure you have moved the decimal point in the right direction and have used an appropriate exponent.

Remember that you can do a quick check with whole numbers to verify that you are using the right rules for variables and exponents.

When adding or subtracting rational expressions, use the rules similar to those for arithmetic of fractions. Find the least common denominator, and then add or subtract as needed.

Real Life Applications of Rational Expressions

Scientists use exponents for scientific notation to express very large or very small numbers. In scientific notation, a number is expressed as $m \times 10^n$, with $1 \le m < 10$. Using scientific notation helps make it easier to work numbers like these.

Rational expressions can be used to determine the amount of resistance in an electrical circuit using Ohm's Law. Current in amperes $(I) = \dfrac{Electricity/volts(E)}{Resistance(R)}$. The formula for finding the current is $I = \dfrac{E}{R}$.

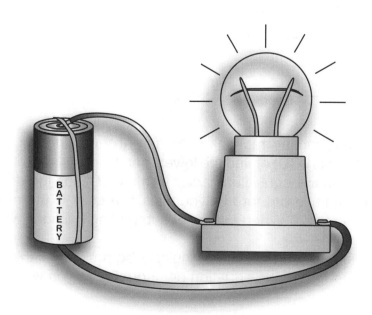

Chapter 6: Roots, Radicals, and Complex Numbers

Introduction to the Concepts of Roots, Radicals, and Complex Numbers

In the last chapter, we found that a rational number is a number that can be expressed as the ratio of two integers. This ratio is sometimes called a fraction. This section will address irrational numbers. Irrational numbers are numbers that cannot be expressed as a ratio.

Concepts of Roots, Radicals, and Complex Numbers

1 Irrational Numbers
2 Roots and Radicals
3 Radical Expressions
4 Real Numbers
5 Complex Numbers

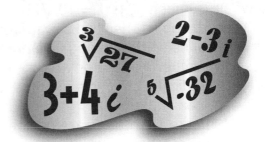

Explanations of the Concepts of Roots, Radicals, and Complex Numbers

1 **Irrational Numbers**

Irrational numbers are numbers that cannot be expressed as a ratio of two integers. The square root of two is an example of an irrational number. An irrational number can be defined as a decimal that never repeats and never ends. The square root of any number that is not a perfect square will be irrational. The square root of 16 or $\sqrt{16}$, which is 4, is a rational number. $\sqrt{3}$ = 1.7320508.... is a decimal that never repeats the same finite block of digits and never ends, so it is an irrational number.

Examples of Irrational Numbers:

$\sqrt{2}$

π is the symbol for pi. The decimal form of pi is 3.1415926 …

0.01011011101111 … is an irrational number because this pattern never ends, and it never repeats the same finite block of digits.

Chapter 6: Roots, Radicals, and Complex Numbers (cont.)

2 Roots and Radicals

A square root of a number is found by finding out what number, multiplied by itself, equals that given number. What number, multiplied by itself, equals 36? The answer is 6 because 6 · 6 = 36. Using an exponent, you could write $6^2 = 36$. The root number in this example is 6. A radical sign $\sqrt{}$ is used as a symbol to mean "find the square root." The question, "what number multiplied by itself equals 36?" can be written symbolically as $\sqrt{36}$. You can check your answer by multiplying the number times itself.

Some numbers are perfect squares. That means that the square root of that number is a whole number. 100, 25, 16, and 9 are all perfect squares because each has a square root that is a whole number. ($\sqrt{100} = 10, \sqrt{25} = 5, \sqrt{16} = 4$, and $\sqrt{9} = 3$).

Every number has two square roots—a positive square root and a negative square root. This is because when two negative numbers are multiplied together, their product or answer is a positive number. For example: -4 · -4 = 16 and 4 · 4 = 16. So is $\sqrt{16}$, the square root of 16, 4 or -4? A radical sign $\sqrt{}$ is used as a symbol to mean "find the principal or positive square root." This means that $\sqrt{16} = 4$.

Numbers such as 3 are not perfect squares because the square root is not a whole number. The symbol ≈, which means "is approximately," is used because the number has been rounded off to provide an estimate of the exact root value. The square root of 3 or $\sqrt{3} ≈$ 1.732. However, if you multiply 1.732 times 1.732 the answer is 2.999824. If the square root is approximated by rounding to the nearest thousandth, it would be 3.000.

Example of a Square Root:

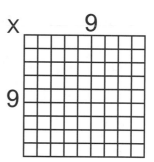

$\sqrt{81} =$ or the square root of 81 = ?

What number times itself equals 81?

9 · 9 = 81

Therefore $\sqrt{81} = 9$

The above example was a perfect square. If the number is not a perfect square, then the square root is not a whole number.

Example of a Number That Is Not a Perfect Square:

$\sqrt{7} ≈ 2.646$

2.646 · 2.646 = 7.001316

Rounded to the nearest hundredth, 7.001316 = 7.00.

Chapter 6: Roots, Radicals, and Complex Numbers (cont.)

Cubed Roots and Higher

Numbers can also have exponents other than 2. For example, when a small three is written to the right of the number n to produce n^3, this means that n is used as a factor 3 times or $n \cdot n \cdot n$. This number reads as "n cubed" or "n raised to the third power." When 3 is cubed or taken to the third power, written as 3^3, multiply 3   3   3 and obtain 27. So three cubed is 27 or $(3^3) = 27$. Scientific notation uses powers of 10. For example, the number 1,000,000 is written as 1 10^6 in scientific notation or 1 times 10   10   10   10   10   10.

Cubed roots can also be found by asking "what number used as a factor three times is equal to the number in question?" The sign for finding the cubed root is $\sqrt[3]{}$. The cube root of 64, written as $\sqrt[3]{64}$, can be thought of as "what number used as a factor three times would produce 64?" The answer is 4   4   4 = 64. Remember that the small number in the crook of the radical sign, in this case 3, is the **index**, and the number under the radical sign, in this case 64, is the **radicand**.

The index can be any number, although we are only going to work with integers or fractions. For example, in $\sqrt[4]{16}$, the index is 4, so what number used as a factor four times produces 16? $\sqrt[4]{16} = 2$ because 2   2   2   2 = 16. This relates to prior work with exponents because we know that $2^4 = 16$.

If n is a positive integer, the general definition used for higher than cubed roots follows. An nth root of b is a solution of the equation $x^n = b$. If n is even and $b > 0$, then there are two real roots of b. The principal root is the positive root. $\sqrt[n]{b}$). The other is the negative root ($-\sqrt[n]{b}$). If n is even and $b = 0$, there is one root ($\sqrt[n]{0} = 0$). If n is even and $b < 0$, there is no real root of b. If n is odd, there is one real root of b, whether b is positive, negative, or zero.

Negative Radicands

When there is a negative radicand, the sign on the root number for the solution is determined by whether the index is odd or even. If the index is an even number, you cannot compute the value. If the index is odd and the radicand is a negative number, the root is a negative number.

Examples of Cubed Roots and Higher:

$\sqrt[3]{n}$ is the sign for finding a cubed root.

$\sqrt[3]{64}$ = What number used as a factor 3 times equals 64?

4   4 = 16 and 16   4 = 64 so 4   4   4 = 64

Using 4 as a factor 3 times equals 64.

$\sqrt[3]{64} = 4$

Chapter 6: Roots, Radicals, and Complex Numbers (cont.)

This notation $\sqrt[x]{n}$ can be used with any index number.

$\sqrt[6]{64}$

The question is "what number used as a factor 6 times equals 64?"

Start from the left and move right since there are no parentheses:

$2 \times 2 = 4$, $4 \times 2 = 8$, $8 \times 2 = 16$, $16 \times 2 = 32$, and $32 \times 2 = 64$
or $2 \times 2 \times 2 \times 2 \times 2 \times 2 = 64$

$\sqrt[6]{64} = 2$ because 2 used as a factor 6 times gives 64.

③ Radical Expressions

Radical expressions with negative radicands can only be solved if the index is an odd number.

Examples of Radical Expressions With Negative Radicands That Can Be Solved:

$\sqrt[3]{-8} = -2$ $\sqrt[5]{-32} = -2$

Examples of Radical Expressions With Negative Radicands That Cannot Be Solved:

$\sqrt[4]{-32}$ The index is even, so it cannot be solved.

Properties of Radicals

Properties of radicals include:

$(\sqrt[n]{b})^n = b$ because $\sqrt[n]{b}$ satisfies the equation $x^n = b$.

$\sqrt[n]{b^n} = b$ if n is odd.

$\sqrt[n]{b^n} = |b|$ if n is even.

Example of the Property $(\sqrt[n]{b})^n = b$ because $\sqrt[n]{b}$ satisfies the equation $x^n = b$:

$(\sqrt{5})^2 = 5$

Chapter 6: Roots, Radicals, and Complex Numbers (cont.)

Example of the Property $\sqrt[n]{b^n} = b$ **if** n **is odd:**

$$\sqrt[3]{9^3} = 9$$

Example of the Property $\sqrt[n]{b^n} = |b|$ **if** n **is even:**

$$\sqrt{(-5)^2} = |-5| = 5$$

Rules for Simplifying Radical Expressions

☐ In simplifying radical expressions, if two numbers are multiplied under the radical sign, you may separate the two expressions. Find the roots of each one and multiply the solutions together.

☐ If two radical expressions are multiplied together, they can be written as a single product under the same radical sign.

☐ You may also find factors for the number under the radical and take the square root of the factors.

☐ If two numbers are divided under a radical sign, they can be separated into two radicals.

☐ Multiplying the numerator and denominator of a radical expression by the same number does not change the value.

☐ Radical expressions can be added and subtracted if each index is the same and each number under the radical sign is the same.

☐ Radical expressions can be written with fractional exponents. The numerator is the power of the number under the radical sign, and the denominator is the number that is the index.

☐ Fractional exponents can be changed into radical expressions. The numerator is the exponent of the number under the radical sign, and the denominator is the index.

☐ Radical expressions are not considered simplified if there is a radical in the denominator.

Examples of the Rules for Simplifying Radical Expressions:

☐ If two numbers are multiplied under the radical sign, you may separate the two expressions.

$$\sqrt{(4)(9)} = (\sqrt{4})(\sqrt{9})$$

Find the square roots of each factor.

$$\sqrt{4} = 2 \qquad \sqrt{9} = 3$$

Chapter 6: Roots, Radicals, and Complex Numbers (cont.)

Multiply the solutions.

$(2)(3) = 6$

$\sqrt{(4)(9)} = 6$

☐ If two radical expressions are multiplied together, they can be written as products under the same radical sign.

$(\sqrt{3})(\sqrt{27}) = \sqrt{(3)(27)} =$

Multiply the numbers under the radical. $3 \quad 27 = 81$

$\sqrt{81} = 9$

$(\sqrt{3})(\sqrt{27}) = 9$

☐ Find factors for the number under the radical and take the square root of the factors.

$\sqrt{18}$

Find the factors of 18. $2 \quad 9$ or $3 \quad 6$

9 is a perfect square, so put the $2 \quad 9$ under the radical sign.

$\sqrt{(2)(9)}$

Remember that parentheses indicate that you should multiply the numbers.

$\sqrt{(2)(9)} = (\sqrt{2})(\sqrt{9})$

$\sqrt{9} = 3$

So $\sqrt{(2)(9)} = 3\sqrt{2}$

You can choose to leave this representation or look for an approximate decimal answer. For the decimal approximation, the square root of 2 is not a whole number, so rounding it to the nearest thousandth, it is ≈ 1.414.

$\sqrt{(2)(9)} \approx 3 \quad 1.414$

Note that this is $\approx$, and not $=$, because the number has been rounded.

☐ If two numbers are divided under a radical sign, they can be separated into two radicals.

$\sqrt{\dfrac{9}{4}}$

Put the numbers under two radical signs. $\dfrac{\sqrt{9}}{\sqrt{4}}$

Chapter 6: Roots, Radicals, and Complex Numbers (cont.)

$\sqrt{9} = 3 \qquad \sqrt{4} = 2$

$\sqrt{\dfrac{9}{4}} = \dfrac{3}{2}$

The properties related to the bullet above are the product and quotient properties of radicals. This property states that if $\sqrt[n]{a}$ and $\sqrt[n]{b}$ are real numbers, then: $\sqrt[n]{ab} = \sqrt[n]{a} \cdot \sqrt[n]{b}$ and $\sqrt[n]{\dfrac{a}{b}} = \dfrac{\sqrt[n]{a}}{\sqrt[n]{b}}$.

Example of $\sqrt[n]{ab} = \sqrt[n]{a} \cdot \sqrt[n]{b}$:

$\sqrt{98} = \sqrt{49 \cdot 2} = \sqrt{49} \cdot \sqrt{2} = 7\sqrt{2}$

Example of $\sqrt[n]{\dfrac{a}{b}} = \dfrac{\sqrt[n]{a}}{\sqrt[n]{b}}$:

$\sqrt[3]{\dfrac{81}{8}} = \dfrac{\sqrt[3]{81}}{\sqrt[3]{8}} = \dfrac{\sqrt[3]{27 \cdot 3}}{2} = \dfrac{\sqrt[3]{27} \cdot \sqrt[3]{3}}{2} = \dfrac{3\sqrt[3]{3}}{2}$

☐ Multiplying the numerator and denominator of a radical expression by the same number will not change the value.

$\dfrac{5}{\sqrt{3}}$

Construct a fraction ($\dfrac{\sqrt{3}}{\sqrt{3}}$) with the same numerator and denominator.

$\dfrac{5}{\sqrt{3}}(\dfrac{\sqrt{3}}{\sqrt{3}}) =$

Remember that a number divided by itself is equal to 1, so the value will not change.

Multiply the expression by the fraction. Put the two square roots in the denominator under the same radical.

$\dfrac{5}{\sqrt{3}}(\dfrac{\sqrt{3}}{\sqrt{3}}) = \dfrac{5\sqrt{3}}{\sqrt{3(3)}} = \dfrac{5\sqrt{3}}{\sqrt{9}}$

Find the square root of the denominator.

$\dfrac{5}{\sqrt{3}} = \dfrac{5\sqrt{3}}{\sqrt{9}} = \dfrac{5\sqrt{3}}{3}$

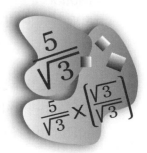

Chapter 6: Roots, Radicals, and Complex Numbers (cont.)

☐ Radical expressions can be added and subtracted if each index is the same and each number under the radical sign (radicand) is the same.

$3\sqrt{4} + 4\sqrt{4} =$

Add the coefficients. $3 + 4 = 7$

Bring the radical over. (Note that this is just like adding $3x + 4x$.)

$3\sqrt{4} + 4\sqrt{4} = 7\sqrt{4} = 7 \cdot 2 = 14$

$2\sqrt[3]{27} + \sqrt[3]{27} =$

Both have the same index and radicand.

Add the coefficients. $2 + 1$

Bring the radical over.

$2\sqrt[3]{27} + \sqrt[3]{27} = 3\sqrt[3]{27} = 3 \cdot 3 = 9$

$3\sqrt[3]{x} - \sqrt[3]{x} =$

Both have the same index and radicand.

Add the coefficients. $3 - 1$

Bring the radical over.

$3\sqrt[3]{x} - \sqrt[3]{x} = 2\sqrt[3]{x}$

☐ Radical expressions can be written as fractional exponents. The numerator is the power of the number under the radical sign, and the denominator is the number that is the index.

$\sqrt[4]{x^3}$

Index $= 4$

Exponent $= 3$

Copy the base under the radical sign. x

Make the numerator the exponent and the denominator the index $= \frac{3}{4}$.

$\sqrt[4]{x^3} = x^{\frac{3}{4}}$

☐ Fractional exponents can be changed into radical expressions. The numerator is the exponent of the number under the radical sign, and the denominator is the index.

$y^{\frac{2}{3}} =$

Write the base under the radical. $\sqrt{y}$

Raise the base the power of the numerator. $\sqrt{y^2}$

Put the denominator as the index. $\sqrt[3]{y^2}$

$y^{\frac{2}{3}} = \sqrt[3]{y^2}$

Chapter 6: Roots, Radicals, and Complex Numbers (cont.)

Rationalizing the Denominator

Rationalizing the denominator is a process that generates the creation of a perfect square, cube, or other power in the denominator, so the radical expression can be written without a fraction in the radicand in the denominator. To rationalize the denominator, multiply the numerator and denominator by the same number to make a perfect square, cube, or other power.

Examples of Rationalizing the Denominator:

$$\sqrt{\frac{3}{5}}$$

Multiply the numerator and denominator by the same number to make a perfect square.

$$\sqrt{\frac{3}{5}} = \sqrt{\frac{3}{5} \cdot \frac{5}{5}} = \sqrt{\frac{15}{25}} = \frac{\sqrt{15}}{\sqrt{25}} = \frac{\sqrt{15}}{5}$$

$$\frac{4}{\sqrt[3]{c}}$$

Multiply the numerator and denominator by the same number to make a perfect cube.

$$\frac{4}{\sqrt[3]{c}} = \frac{4(\sqrt[3]{c^2})}{\sqrt[3]{c}(\sqrt[3]{c^2})} = \frac{4\sqrt[3]{c^2}}{\sqrt[3]{c^3}} = \frac{4\sqrt[3]{c^2}}{c}$$

Simplifying Like Radicals

Like radicals have the same index and radicand. Using the distributive property, you can add or subtract like radicals. When you combine like radicals, you may have to simplify them first.

Examples of Simplifying Like Radicals:

$$\sqrt{8} + \sqrt{98} = \sqrt{2 \cdot 4} + \sqrt{2 \cdot 49} = 2\sqrt{2} + 7\sqrt{2} = 9\sqrt{2}$$

$$\frac{\sqrt{21} + \sqrt{15}}{\sqrt{3}} = \frac{\sqrt{21}}{\sqrt{3}} + \frac{\sqrt{15}}{\sqrt{3}} = \sqrt{7} + \sqrt{5}$$

Chapter 6: Roots, Radicals, and Complex Numbers (cont.)

Multiplying Bionomials With Radicals

Binomials with radicals can be multiplied just like binomials were multiplied using FOIL or by just multiplying the second factor by each of the expressions in the first factor and adding them together.

Example of Multiplying Binomials With Radicals:

$$(4 + \sqrt{7})(3 + 2\sqrt{7})$$
$$4(3 + 2\sqrt{7}) + \sqrt{7}(3 + 2\sqrt{7})$$
$$12 + 8\sqrt{7} + 3\sqrt{7} + 2(\sqrt{7})^2$$
$$12 + 11\sqrt{7} + 2(7)$$
$$12 + 11\sqrt{7} + 14$$
$$26 + 11\sqrt{7}$$

Solving Equations With Radicals With Square Roots

In solving equations with radicals involving square roots, start by isolating the radical term on one side of the equation. Square both sides of the equation. If solving radical equations with cube roots, then cube both sides of the equation. Always check to see if your solution works, as sometimes this process introduces a solution for an equation that does not solve the equation with which you started. In this case, we say we have found an **extraneous solution**.

Example of Solving Radical Equations With Square Roots:

$$\sqrt{2x - 1} = 3$$

Step 1: Isolate the radical.

$\sqrt{2x - 1} = 3$ The radical is already isolated.

Step 2: Square both sides.

$(\sqrt{2x - 1})^2 = 3^2$

$2x - 1 = 9$

Step 3: Solve.

$2x - 1 = 9$

$2x - 1 + 1 = 9 + 1$

$2x = 10$

$\dfrac{2x}{2} = \dfrac{10}{2}$

Answer: $x = 5$

Step 4: Check the results.

$\sqrt{2x - 1} = 3$

$\sqrt{2(5) - 1} = 3$

$\sqrt{10 - 1} = 3$

$\sqrt{9} = 3$

$3 = 3$

The answer is correct.

Chapter 6: Roots, Radicals, and Complex Numbers (cont.)

Example of Solving Radical Equations Cube Roots:

$2\sqrt[3]{x} - 1 = 3$

Step 1: Isolate the radical.

$2\sqrt[3]{x} - 1 = 3$

$2\sqrt[3]{x} - 1 + 1 = 3 + 1$

$2\sqrt[3]{x} = 4$

Step 2: Cube both sides.

$(2\sqrt[3]{x})^3 = 4^3$

$8x = 64$

Step 3: Solve.

$8x = 64$

$\dfrac{8x}{8} = \dfrac{64}{8}$

Answer: $x = 8$

Step 4: Check the answer.

$2\sqrt[3]{x} - 1 = 3$

$2\sqrt[3]{8} - 1 = 3$

$2(2) - 1 = 3$

$4 - 1 = 3$

$3 = 3$

The answer is correct.

Solving Linear Equations With Radicals

When solving linear equations with radicals, it is not necessary to square both sides. Just use the usual algebraic ideas and rules discussed above to generate the solution.

Example of Solving a Linear Equation With a Radical:

$3x = 2 + x\sqrt{5}$

Step 1: Isolate the radical.

$3x - x\sqrt{5} = 2 + x\sqrt{5} - x\sqrt{5}$

$3x - x\sqrt{5} = 2$

Step 2: Solve the equation.

Chapter 6: Roots, Radicals, and Complex Numbers (cont.)

$$x(3 - \sqrt{5}) = 2$$

$$\frac{x(3 - \sqrt{5})}{(3 - \sqrt{5})} = \frac{2}{(3 - \sqrt{5})}$$

$$x = \frac{2}{(3 - \sqrt{5})}$$

$$x = \frac{2}{(3 - \sqrt{5})} \cdot \frac{3 + \sqrt{5}}{3 + \sqrt{5}}$$

$$x = \frac{2(3 + \sqrt{5})}{9 - 5}$$

$$x = \frac{6 + 2\sqrt{5}}{4}$$

$$x = \frac{3 + \sqrt{5}}{2}$$

④ Real Numbers

Real numbers are a combination of all the number systems. Real numbers include natural numbers, whole numbers, integers, rational numbers, and irrational numbers. The **completeness property of real numbers** states that every real number has a decimal representation, and every decimal represents a real number. To find the decimal representation of a rational number, use division until you find a finite or terminating decimal.

Example of Finding the Decimal Representation of a Rational Number:

$\frac{13}{2} = 13 \div 2 = 6.5 =$ terminating decimal

$\frac{19}{22} = 19 \div 22 = 0.8636363 \ldots =$ repeating decimal

This can also be written as $0.8\overline{63}$, showing that the 63 continues to repeat.

88

Chapter 6: Roots, Radicals, and Complex Numbers (cont.)

The decimal representation of a rational number is either terminating or repeating, and every repeating or terminating decimal represents a rational number. The decimal representation of an irrational number is always infinite and nonrepeating, and every infinite and nonrepeating decimal represents an irrational number.

Examples of Irrational Numbers:

(Note that we might not be able to see that it is nonrepeating.)

$\pi = 3.14159265 \dots$

$\sqrt{3} = 1.7320508 \dots$

There is no solution for $x^2 + 1$ because the square of a real number is never negative. Hence, $x = \sqrt{-1}$ was considered an **imaginary number**. However, the solution $x = \sqrt{-1}$ is called i. Imaginary numbers of the form of bi with $b \neq 0$ are called **pure imaginary numbers**.

5 ## Complex Numbers

The system that includes imaginary numbers is called the complex number system. When pure imaginary numbers are combined with real numbers, imaginary numbers for the form $a + bi$ ($b \neq 0$) are the result. These combined real and imaginary numbers form the set of **complex numbers**. Two complex numbers are equal only if they have equal real parts and equal imaginary parts. The equality of complex numbers states $a + bi = c + di$ if and only if $a = c$ and $b = d$. The sum of two complex numbers is defined as $(a + bi) + (c + di) = (a + c) + (b + d)i$. That is, we add or subtract real and imaginary numbers by combining the real parts and combining the imaginary parts separately.

Example of Adding or Subtracting Complex Numbers:

$(3 + 6i) + (4 - 2i)$
$(3 + 4) + (6 - 2)i$
$7 + (4)i$

Chapter 6: Roots, Radicals, and Complex Numbers (cont.)

The product of two complex numbers is defined as $(a + bi)(c + di) = (ac - bd) + (ad + bc)i$. Multiply two complex numbers like multiplying any two binomials, and remember to use the fact that $x^2 = -1$.

$$(3 + 4i)(5 + 2i)$$
$$3(5 + 2i) + 4i(5 + 2i)$$
$$15 + 6i + 20i + 8i^2$$
$$15 + 26i + 8(-1)$$
$$15 + 26i - 8$$
$$7 + 26i$$

The complex numbers $a + bi$ and $a - bi$ are called **conjugates**, and their product is $a^2 + b^2$. To simplify the quotient of two complex numbers, multiply the numerator and denominator by the conjugate of the denominator, much like in rationalizing a denominator.

Example of Simplifying an Expression by Multiplying by the Conjugate:

$$\frac{5 - i}{2 + 3i}$$

Step 1:   Multiply by the conjugate of the denominator.

$$\frac{5 - i}{2 + 3i} \cdot \frac{2 - 3i}{2 - 3i}$$

$$\frac{5(2 - 3i) - i(2 - 3i)}{2(2 - 3i) + 3i(2 - 3i)}$$

$$\frac{10 - 15i - 2i + 3i^2}{4 - 6i + 6i - 9i^2}$$

$$\frac{10 - 17i + 3i^2}{4 - 9i^2}$$

Step 2:   Solve the equation.

$$\frac{10 - 17i + 3i^2}{4 - 9i^2}$$

$$\frac{10 - 17i - 3}{4 + 9}$$

$$\frac{7 - 17i}{13} = \frac{7}{13} - \frac{17i}{13}$$

90

Name: _____ Date: _____

Chapter 6: Roots, Radicals, and Complex Numbers (cont.)

Practice: Roots, Radicals, and Complex Numbers

Roots and Radicals
Simplify. Show your work.

1. $\sqrt{\dfrac{1}{64}}$

2. $\sqrt[3]{a^6}$

3. $\sqrt{13^6}$

Products and Quotients
Simplify. Show your work.

4. $\sqrt{\dfrac{50}{49}}$ = _____

5. $\sqrt[3]{\dfrac{2}{9}}$ = _____

6. $\sqrt{6} \cdot \sqrt{\dfrac{2}{3}}$ = _____

7. $\sqrt[3]{\dfrac{27a}{4b^4}}$ = _____

Sums of Radicals
Simplify. Show your work.

8. $\sqrt{50} + \sqrt{18}$ = _____

9. $\sqrt{6} + \sqrt{36} + \sqrt{216}$ = _____

10. $\sqrt{\dfrac{27}{5}} - \sqrt{\dfrac{3}{5}}$ = _____

11. $\dfrac{\sqrt[3]{18} + 3\sqrt[3]{54}}{\sqrt[3]{3}}$ = _____

Name: _____ Date: _____

Chapter 6: Roots, Radicals, and Complex Numbers (cont.)

Simplify the binomials with radicals. Show your work on your own paper.

12. $(2\sqrt{3} - \sqrt{6})^2$ = _____

13. $(4\sqrt{5} + 3\sqrt{2})(4\sqrt{5} - 3\sqrt{2})$ = _____

14. $\dfrac{3 + \sqrt{5}}{3 - \sqrt{5}}$ = _____

Solve the equations with radicals. Show your work on your own paper.

15. $3x - 5\sqrt{x} = 2$ Solution = _____

16. $2\sqrt[3]{x} = \sqrt[3]{x^2}$ Solution = _____

Solve the radical equations and linear radical equations. Show your work on your own paper.

17. $5\sqrt{x} = 10$ Solution = _____

18. $x\sqrt{5} = 10$ Solution = _____

Decimal Representation
Write each fraction as a decimal.

19. $\frac{5}{8}$ = _____

20. $\frac{13}{7}$ = _____

21. $\frac{13}{4}$ = _____

Complex Numbers
Simplify. Show your work on your own paper.

22. $(3 + 6i) - (4 - 2i)$ = _____

23. $(3 + 4i)^2$ = _____

24. $\dfrac{2}{3 - i}$ = _____

Chapter 6: Roots, Radicals, and Complex Numbers (cont.)

Summary of Roots, Radicals, and Complex Numbers

The exponent tells how many times the number is used as a factor. Square roots are found by finding out what number used as a factor twice equals the number in question. Finding the cube root is written as $\sqrt[3]{n}$. The question is "what number used as a factor 3 times will equal n?" Higher roots will be represented by $\sqrt[x]{n}$ where x is the variable representing the index of the root, and n is the radicand for which you are finding the root.

To solve equations with radicals: isolate the radical, square both sides if it is a square root, or cube both sides if it is a cube root, and solve the equation.

Imaginary numbers have the form of bi with $b \neq 0$, and are called pure imaginary numbers.

Combined real and imaginary numbers form the set of complex numbers. The equality of complex numbers states that $a + bi = c + di$ if an only if $a = c$ and $b = d$. The sum of two complex numbers is defined as $(a + bi) + (c + di) = (a + c) + (b + d)i$. Add or subtract real and imaginary numbers by combining the real parts and combining the imaginary parts separately.

The product of two complex numbers is defined as $(a + bi)(c + di) = (ac - bd) + (ad + bc)i$.

Tips to Remember

☐ Remember what simplified form means. We usually want the numbers to be written without complex numbers or radicals in the denominator.

☐ The FOIL method is employed when rationalizing a denominator with a binomial or complex number. (The FOIL method is an easy way to remember the necessary steps to complete the multiplication: multiply the **F**irst terms, **O**utside terms, **I**nside terms, and then the **L**ast terms.)

☐ Solving equations can be enhanced by squaring or cubing both sides of an equation, although this might introduce an extraneous solution.

• Checking your solutions is always important.

☐ When changing a fraction to a decimal form, make sure you have done enough divisions to determine the repeating part.

Real Life Applications of Roots, Radicals, and Complex Numbers

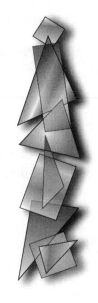

Squares and square roots are used in finding the surface area of a square or the length of the sides. If you know the surface area of the square, that could help you find out how much paint is needed for a certain area. Skydivers use radical equations to find the velocity of freefalling using the formula $v = \sqrt{2gd}$.

If a square has a side with the length of x, the length of a diagonal of the square is $\sqrt{2}$. In a triangle with angles of 30, 60, and 90 degrees, if the shortest side has the length x, then the side opposite the 60-degree angle has the length of $x\sqrt{3}$.

Chapter 7: Quadratic Equations and Functions

Introduction to the Concepts of Quadratic Equations and Functions

Quadratic equations are equations that include a term where the variable is raised to the second power (has an exponent of 2). It is written in the general form of $ax^2 + bx + c$, where a, b, and c are real numbers and $a \neq 0$. The quadratic formula can be used to find the roots of the quadratic equation. A function is called quadratic if it is of the form, $f(x) = ax^2 + bx + c$, where a, b, and c are real numbers and $a \neq 0$. Because of the exponent on the lead term, ax^2, quadratic functions are degree two polynomial functions.

Concepts of Quadratic Equations and Functions

1   Solving Quadratic Equations

2   Roots of Quadratic Equations

3   General Form of Quadratic Functions

4   Graphing Quadratic Functions

Explanations of the Concepts of Quadratic Equations and Functions

1   **Solving Quadratic Equations**

Quadratic equations are equations that include a term where the variable is raised to the second power (has an exponent of 2). In addition, no other term can include the variable raised to a higher power. The general form of a quadratic equation is $ax^2 + bx + c = 0$, where a, b, and c can be any real number that does not equal 0.

Examples of Quadratic Equations:

$$2x^2 - 3x + 1 = 0 \qquad -5x^2 + 7 = 0 \qquad \tfrac{1}{2}x^2 + x = 0$$

Quadratic equations can be solved by using one or more of these methods: factoring, completing the square, or using the quadratic formula.

Chapter 7: Quadratic Equations and Functions (cont.)

Quadratic equations can also be formed when a linear equation is multiplied by the variable in the equation.

Example of Forming a Quadratic Equation From a Linear Equation by Multiplying the Linear Equation by the Variable in the Equation:

$a(a + 8)$
$(a \bullet a) + (a \bullet 8)$
$a(a + 8) = a^2 + 8a$

Quadratic equations can also be formed when two binomial expressions are multiplied together. There are five steps to multiply two binomial expressions.

Step 1: Multiply the two first terms.

Step 2: Multiply the two outside terms.

Step 3: Multiply the two inside terms.

Step 4: Multiply the two last terms.

Step 5: Add the terms together.

Example of Forming a Quadratic Equation By Multiplying Two Binomial Expressions:

Problem: $(y - 5)(y - 3)$

Step 1: Multiply the two first terms. $y \bullet y = y^2$

Step 2: Multiply the two outside terms. $y \bullet -3 = -3y$

Step 3: Multiply the two inside terms. $-5 \bullet y = -5y$

Step 4: Multiply the two last terms. $-5 \bullet -3 = 15$

Step 5: Add the terms together. $y^2 - 3y - 5y + 15 = y^2 - 8y + 15$

Answer: $(y - 5)(y - 3) = y^2 - 8y + 15$

When multiplying binomial expressions, multiply the **First** terms, **Outside** terms, **Inside** terms, and then the **Last** terms. **FOIL** is an easy way to remember the necessary steps to complete the multiplication.

95

Chapter 7: Quadratic Equations and Functions (cont.)

Solving Quadratic Equations by Factoring

The easiest way of solving quadratic equations is by factoring. To factor a quadratic equation, it must first be put into standard form and then simplified. The standard form of a quadratic equation is $ax^2 + bx + c = 0$ where $a \neq 0$.

Example of Putting an Equation in Standard Form:

$3x^2 - 7x = 4$
Put into standard form by adding or subtracting the same terms from both sides of the equation. $3x^2 - 7x - 4 = 4 - 4$
Simplify. $3x^2 - 7x - 4 = 0$

Now that the equation is in standard form, the quadratic equation can be solved by factoring. There are three types of quadratic equations in standard form. Type I has only two terms and has the form of $ax^2 + c = 0$. Type I does not include an x term. Type II has only two terms and has the form $ax^2 + bx = 0$. Type II does not include a constant term (the number term). Type III quadratic equations have all three terms and have the form $ax^2 + bx + c = 0$ where $a \neq 0$. How to use factoring to solve each of these three types of standard form quadratic equations will be shown in the following examples.

Example of Solving Type I Quadratic Equations in Standard Form by Factoring:

Problem: $a^2 - 49 = 0$

Step 1:   Add or subtract to move the a^2 term to one side of the equation.
$a^2 - 49 + 49 = 49 + 0$
$a^2 - 0 = 49$

Step 2:   Multiply or divide to eliminate the coefficient in front of the a. In this case, the coefficient is one, so $1 \bullet a^2 = a^2$.
$a^2 = 49$

Step 3:   Take the square root of both sides of the equal signs.
$\sqrt{a^2} = \sqrt{49}$
$(a - 7)(a + 7) = 0$

$a - 7 = 0$	$a + 7 = 0$
$a - 7 + 7 = 0 + 7$	$a + 7 - 7 = 0 - 7$

Answers: $a = 7$ or $a = $-$7$

Step 4:   Check your answer by replacing the a with 7 and -7.

$7^2 - 49 = 0$	$(\text{-}7)^2 - 49 = 0$
$7^2 = 7 \quad 7 = 49$	$(\text{-}7)^2 = \text{-}7 \quad \text{-}7 = 49$
$49 - 49 = 0$	$49 - 49 = 0$
$0 = 0$	$0 = 0$

Chapter 7: Quadratic Equations and Functions (cont.)

Example of Solving Type II Quadratic Equations in Standard Form by Factoring:

Problem: $x^2 + 10x = 0$

Step 1:   Factor an x out of the equation.
$x(x + 10) = 0$

Step 2:   Set both factors equal to zero.
$x = 0$ $x + 10 = 0$

Step 3:   Solve both equations.

Answer 1: $x = 0$ $x + 10 = 0$
$x + 10 - 10 = 0 - 10$
$x + 0 = \text{-}10$

Answer 2: $x = \text{-}10$

Step 4:   Check your answers by substituting the value
of x in the original equation.
$x^2 + 10x = 0$ $x^2 + 10x = 0$
$(0)^2 + 10(0) = 0$ $(\text{-}10)^2 + 10(\text{-}10) = 0$
Simplify.   Simplify.
$0 + 0 = 0$ $100 + (\text{-}100) = 0$
$0 = 0$ $0 = 0$

Example of Solving Type III Quadratic Equations in Standard Form by Factoring:

Step 1:   Put the equation in standard form.
$x^2 - 5x + 4 = 0$

Step 2:   Factor the x^2 term.
$x^2 = (x)(x)$
$(x\quad)(x\quad) = 0$

Step 3:   List pairs of factors in numerical term.
Numerical term is 4, so factors could be:
$(2)(2) = 4$
$(\text{-}2)(\text{-}2) = 4$
$(\text{-}1)(\text{-}4) = 4$
$(1)(4) = 4$
$4 = 4$

Chapter 7: Quadratic Equations and Functions (cont.)

Step 4:   Place one pair of factors in parentheses. Check to see if multiplying the two binomial expressions results in the original equation. (**Note:** use FOIL). If not, try another pair of factors until the correct pair is found.

$(x + 2)(x + 2) = 0$

First terms:
$(x)(x) = x^2$
Outside terms:
$(x)(2) = 2x$
Inside terms:
$(2)(x) = 2x$
Last terms:
$(2)(2) = 4$
Add them all together.
$x^2 + 2x + 2x + 4$
$x^2 + 4x + 4 = 0$

Step 5:   Not the original equation, so try another pair.
$(x - 4)(x - 1) = 0$

First terms:
$(x)(x) = x^2$
Outside terms:
$(x)(-4) = -4x$
Inside terms:
$(-1)(x) = -1x$
Last terms:
$(-4)(-1) = 4$
Add them all together.
$x^2 - 4x - 1x + 4$
Simplify.
$x^2 - 5x + 4 = 0$

This is the original equation.
$x^2 - 5x + 4 = 0$

Step 6:   Set each binomial expression equal to zero.
$x - 4 = 0$ $x - 1 = 0$

Chapter 7: Quadratic Equations and Functions (cont.)

Step 7:   Solve each equation.

$x - 4 = 0$ $x - 1 = 0$

$x - 4 + 4 = 0 + 4$ $x - 1 + 1 = 0 + 1$

Answers: $x = 4$ $x = 1$

Step 8:   Check the answer.
Substitute 4 in the original equation.

$x^2 - 5x + 4 = 0$

$4^2 - 5(4) + 4 = 0$

$16 - 20 + 4 = 0$

$0 = 0$, so $x = 4$ is correct.

Now substitute the 1 in the equation.

$x^2 - 5x + 4 = 0$

$1^2 - (5)(1) + 4$

$1 - 5 + 4 = 0$

$-4 + 4 = 0$

$0 = 0$, so $x = 1$ is correct.

Solving Quadratic Equations by Completing the Square

When a quadratic equation does not resolve into a factored form, it can be resolved by completing the square. Completing the square method works by finding a constant quantity (a number) that is added to both sides of the equation to make it look like a perfect square.

Example of Completing the Square Method to Solve a Quadratic Equation:

Problem: $x^2 + 2x = 1$

Step 1:   Make it look like a perfect square by adding 1 to both sides.

$x^2 + 2x + 1 = 1 + 1$

$x^2 + 2x + 1 = 2$

Step 2:   The equation can now be factored.

$(x + 1)^2 = 2$

Step 3:   Solution can be found by taking the square root of each side.

$\sqrt{(x + 1)^2} = \pm\sqrt{2}$

So

$x + 1 = \pm\sqrt{2}$

$x + 1 - 1 = \pm\sqrt{2} - 1$

$x = -1 \pm\sqrt{2}$

Answers: $x = -1 + \sqrt{2}$ or $x = -1 - \sqrt{2}$ are the two solutions for the equation.

Chapter 7: Quadratic Equations and Functions (cont.)

Solving Quadratic Equations Using the Quadratic Formula

Quadratic equations can also be solved using the Quadratic Formula. This is a method for solving quadratic equations that will always work. First put the formula in standard form $ax^2 + bx + c = 0$. Identify the values of a, b, and c. Substitute the values for a, b, and c into the formula, and solve it. Then check your answer. Using the quadratic formula, you may get zero, one, or two answers that are real numbers.

Quadratic Formula

For any equation of the form $ax^2 + bx + c = 0$, the solutions to the equation are given by:

$$x = \frac{-b \pm \sqrt{b^2 - 4ac}}{2a}$$

Example of Solving a Quadratic Equation With the Quadratic Formula:

Problem: $x^2 + 2x + 1 = 0$

Step 1: Put the quadratic equation in standard form. $ax^2 + bx + c = 0$. This equation is in standard form.

$$x^2 + 2x + 1 = 0$$

Step 2: Find the values of a, b, c.
x^2 has the coefficient of 1, so $a = 1$.
$2x$ has the coefficient of 2, so $b = 2$.
The number in the equation is 1, so $c = 1$.

Step 3: Substitute a, b, and c into the quadratic formula.
Quadratic Formula: **Substitutions:**

$$x = \frac{-b \pm \sqrt{b^2 - 4ac}}{2a} \qquad x = \frac{-2 \pm \sqrt{2^2 - 4(1)(1)}}{2(1)}$$

Step 4: Compute the values under the radical sign first.

$$\frac{-2 \pm \sqrt{2^2 - 4(1)(1)}}{2(1)} = \frac{-2 \pm \sqrt{4 - 4}}{2(1)} = \frac{-2 \pm \sqrt{0}}{2(1)} = \frac{-2 \pm 0}{2(1)} = \frac{-2}{2} = -1$$

Answer: $x = -1$

Chapter 7: Quadratic Equations and Functions (cont.)

Step 5:   Check the answer. Substitute -1 into the original equation.
$x^2 + 2x + 1$
$= (-1)^2 + 2(-1) + 1$
$= 1 + (-2) + 1$
$= -1 + 1$
$= 0$

So $x = -1$ is the correct answer, and there is only one solution.
$x^2 + 2x + 1 = 0$ when $x = -1$

Quadratic Equation Applications/Problem Solving

Quadratic equations can be used to solve everyday problems. If you were trying to carpet a rectangular room, you can use a quadratic equation to solve the problem.

Problem: The width of a rectangular room is 10 meters less than the length of the room. The surface area of the floor in the room is 600 square meters. What are the length and the width of the floor in the room?

Step 1:   What is known?
The width of the room is 10 meters less than the length.
Use L to represent the length, so the width is $(L - 10)$.

To find the surface area, multiply the length times the width.
So $L(L - 10)$ is the area of the floor.

The area of the floor was 600 square meters.
So $L(L - 10) = 600$ square meters.

Step 2:   Multiply the equation.
$L^2 - 10L = 600$ square meters

Step 3:   Put the equation in standard form $ax^2 + bx + c = 0$.
$L^2 - 10L - 600 = 600 - 600$
$L^2 - 10L - 600 = 0$

Step 4:   Factor the equation.
$(L - 30)(L + 20) = 0$

Step 5:   Solve for L.
If $L - 30 = 0$, then $L = 30$.
If $L + 20 = 0$, then $L = -20$.

Chapter 7: Quadratic Equations and Functions (cont.)

Answer: The length of the floor cannot be a negative number, so the length must be 30 meters.
The width is $L - 10$, so $30 - 10 = 20$, so the width = 20 meters.

Check: Surface area is the length times the width, and the surface area of the room is 600 square meters.
(30 meters)(20 meters) = 600 square meters, so the answer is correct.

② Roots of Quadratic Equations

The quadratic formula can be used to find the roots of the quadratic equation. The standard form of a quadratic equation is $ax^2 + bx + c = 0$.

The quadratic formula is $x = \dfrac{-b \pm \sqrt{b^2 - 4ac}}{2a}$ if $a \neq 0$.

$ax^2 + bx + c = 0$ is a quadratic equation with real coefficients. The term $b^2 - ac$ is called the **discriminant**, **D**. If $b^2 - 4ac > 0$, then there are two different real roots. If $b^2 - 4ac = 0$, then there is a real double root. If $b^2 - 4ac < 0$, then there are two complex conjugate roots. A **discriminant** discriminates among the three cases above. A discriminant shows whether or not the quadratic equation with integral coefficients has rational roots. Integral coefficients are rational numbers. A quadratic equation has rational roots if: the quadratic equation has integral coefficients and its discriminant is a perfect square or if the quadratic equation can be transformed into an equivalent equation that meets the first requirement.

Example of Determining the Nature of the Roots:

$3x^2 - 7x + 5 = 0$

$D = b^2 - 4ac$

$D = (-7)^2 - 4(3)(5)$

$D = 49 - 60$

$D = -11$

This is a negative number, so the roots are complex conjugates.

Chapter 7: Quadratic Equations and Functions (cont.)

③ General Form of a Quadratic Function

Just as linear functions all have the same general form, the next class of functions called **quadratic functions** will all have the same general form. A function is called quadratic if it is of the form, $f(x) = ax^2 + bx + c$, where a, b, and c are real numbers and $a \neq 0$. Note that $f(x) = ax^2 + bx + c$ is the same as $y = ax^2 + bx + c$. It is just a different representation of the same idea. Because of the exponent on the lead term, ax^2, quadratic functions are degree two polynomial functions.

Examples of Quadratic Functions:

$$f(x) = x^2 + 3x + 4$$
$$g(t) = -2t^2 + 7$$
$$h(x) = \tfrac{2}{3}x^2 + 6x$$

④ Graphing a Quadratic Function

One approach to graphing a quadratic function is to set up a table, pick some inputs for x, and compute the related outputs. Then take your ordered pairs from the table, plot them on the coordinate system, and connect the points to form the graph. For example, suppose we want to graph the quadratic function, $f(x) = x^2$. Remember that $f(x) = x^2$ is just a different representation of $y = x^2$. The table below shows one choice of ordered pairs that could be used to sketch the graph of the function. The resulting graph reveals a shape called a **parabola**.

x	y
-2	4
-1	1
2	4
0	0
1	1

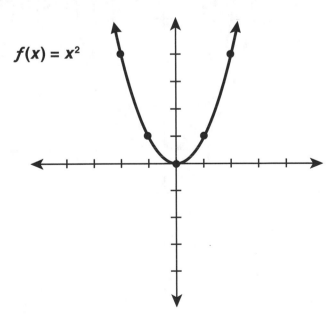

$f(x) = x^2$

Chapter 7: Quadratic Equations and Functions (cont.)

It is easy to tell whether the graph of the quadratic function, $f(x) = ax^2 + bx + c$, will be a parabola opening up or opening down. Look at the coefficient a of the ax^2 term of the function rule. If a is positive, the parabola opens up (holding water like a bowl), and if a is negative, the parabola opens down (shedding water like an umbrella). So, the graph of $g(x) = -x^2$ is the mirror image of $f(x) = x^2$. It is the same parabola, just opening down rather than opening up as is seen in the figure at the right. Note: $f(x) = (-x)^2$ is not the same as $g(x) = -x^2$.

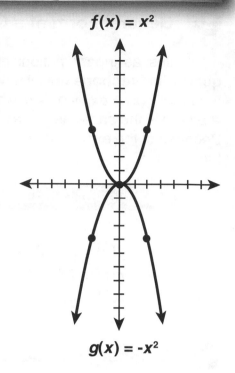

$f(x) = x^2$

$g(x) = -x^2$

What other information can a, the coefficient on the ax^2 term, provide? To investigate, let's graph three different quadratic functions on the same coordinate system and look to see what happens. For this example, the functions to graph are:

$$f(x) = x^2 \qquad g(x) = 2x^2 \qquad h(x) = \tfrac{1}{2}x^2$$

By plotting the points shown, the graphs of the three functions are as seen.

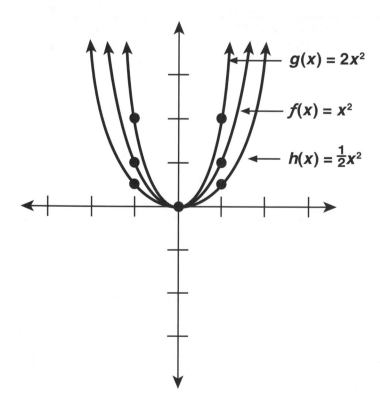

$g(x) = 2x^2$

$f(x) = x^2$

$h(x) = \tfrac{1}{2}x^2$

Let's consider the graph of the function $f(x) = x^2$ as the basic parabola. How does putting a 2 as the coefficient on x^2 change the basic parabola? Since the graph of $g(x) = 2x^2$ falls inside our basic parabola, the 2 has made the parabola narrower. What about using a value for the coefficient that is less than one? Note that the graph of $h(x) = \tfrac{1}{2}x^2$ falls outside the basic parabola. The fractional value causes the parabola to widen or broaden from the basic x^2 shape. The role of a, the coefficient on x^2, tells two valuable pieces of information for graphing a quadratic function of the form, $f(x) = ax^2 + bx + c$. First, if $a > 0$, then the parabola opens up, and if $a < 0$, the parabola will open down. Second, if $a > 1$, the parabola will be narrower than the general x^2 parabola, and if $0 < a < 1$, the parabola will be wider than the general x^2 parabola.

104

Chapter 7: Quadratic Equations and Functions (cont.)

Examples:

Function	Parabola Opens	Narrower or Wider
$f(x) = -5x^2 + 7$	Down	Narrower
$g(t) = 0.25t^2 - 5t + 3$	Up	Wider

Vertex

Now that several examples of simple quadratic functions have been seen, it is clear what a parabola looks like. What other important characteristic would it be helpful to have to quickly and efficiently draw the graph of a quadratic function? How about knowing the high point or maximum height for the graph (if the parabola opens down) or the low point or minimum height for the graph (if the parabola opens up)? Wouldn't that make graphing a parabola easier? It turns out that we can find this point called the **vertex** of the parabola.

The vertex of the parabola defined by the quadratic function of the form, $f(x) = ax^2 + bx + c$, where a, b, and c are real numbers and $a \neq 0$, is found with the x-coordinate, which is $\left(\dfrac{-b}{2a}\right)$. The y-coordinate is found by substituting the coordinate x value into the equation $f\left(\dfrac{-b}{2a}\right)$, so the vertex is at the point $\left(\dfrac{-b}{2a}, f\left(\dfrac{-b}{2a}\right)\right)$. So, based on the coefficients for the x^2 and x terms, we can determine the x-coordinate for the vertex and then evaluate the function for that value of x to get the y-coordinate for the vertex.

Example:

Step 1: Consider the quadratic function, $f(x) = -2x^2 + 6x + 1$. Find the vertex.

Step 2: The x-coordinate is 1.5 because $a = -2$ and $b = 6$. $\dfrac{-6}{2(-2)} = \dfrac{-6}{-4} = 1.5$

Step 3: The y-coordinate is $f(1.5) = -2(1.5)^2 + 6(1.5) + 1 = 5.5$.

Step 4: The vertex for the parabola will be at the point (1.5, 5.5). Since the coefficient on x^2 is -2, the parabola will open down from this point since the coefficient on x^2 is a negative number.

x- and *y*-intercepts

To complete the graph of a quadratic function, it is helpful to find the x-intercept(s) and the y-intercept for the graph. Let's start with the y-intercept. To find the y-intercept for the function $f(x) = ax^2 + bx + c$, just let $x = 0$ and find the value for $f(0)$. Note that this will always be the value c! This means that the point $(0, c)$ will be a point on the graph of the parabola.

Chapter 7: Quadratic Equations and Functions (cont.)

The graph of a quadratic function might not intersect the x-axis at all; it might touch at one point (think of $f(x) = x^2$ touching only at (0, 0)), or it might intersect the x-axis at two points. To find the x-intercept(s) for the graph of $f(x) = ax^2 + bx + c$, we can use what we learned about solving quadratic equations. Namely, we can use factoring or the quadratic formula to locate the x-intercept value(s). To do this, set the given quadratic function equal to 0 and solve for x.

Example:

Problem: $f(x) = x^2 + x - 12$

Step 1:   Find the y-intercept: Let $x = 0$, find $f(0) = 0^2 + 0 - 12 = -12$, so the point (0, -12) is on the parabola.

Step 2:   Find the x-intercept: Let $y = f(x) = 0$ and solve for x.
$0 = x^2 + x - 12$ Try factoring as the first method of solution.
$0 = (x - 3)(x + 4)$
$0 = x - 3$ or $0 = x + 4$
$x = 3$ or $x = -4$

This means that the parabola will intersect the x-axis in two points (3, 0) and (-4, 0).

Step 3:   What would the vertex for this parabola be? $x = -\frac{1}{2} = -0.5$
(by substitution in $x = \frac{-b}{2a}$).

Step 4:   And $f(-\frac{1}{2}) = (-\frac{1}{2})^2 + (-\frac{1}{2}) - 12 = -\frac{49}{4} = -12.25$
so the vertex point is $(-\frac{1}{2}, -\frac{49}{4})$ or (-0.5, -12.25).

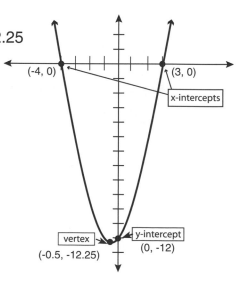

Step 5:   Does the parabola open up or down? Up, because the coefficient on x^2 is positive.

Step 6:   All of this information can now be used to draw the graph for the quadratic function in the example.

Name: _____ Date: _____

Chapter 7: Quadratic Equations and Functions (cont.)

Practice: Quadratic Equations

For this activity, use your own scratch paper to work the problems.

Form a quadratic equation from a linear equation by the variable in the equation for questions 1–3.

1. $x(5x + 8) = 0$

2. $-a(10a - 2) = 0$

3. $4x(2x - 3) = -3$

_____   _____   _____

Form a quadratic equation by multiplying binomial expressions for questions 4 and 5.

4. $(2c - 5)(3c + 1) = 0$

5. $(x + 2)(x - 3) = 0$

_____   _____

Use factoring to solve questions 6–8.

6. $3x^2 - 27 = 0$

7. $2a^2 - 6a = 0$

8. $2b^2 + 7b = -6$

_____   _____   _____

Use the complete the square method to solve question 9.

9. $x^2 + 6x + 7 = 0$ _____

Use the quadratic formula to solve questions 10 and 11.

10. $2x^2 + 5x + 2 = 0$

11. $3x^2 + x - 2 = 0$

_____   _____

Solve using a quadratic equation.

12. Ian wanted to build a dog pen for his new beagle. He used the wall of the house for one side. He bought 20 meters of fence to build the other 3 sides. Find the dimensions of the pen if the area is 48 square meters.

_____

Without solving, determine the nature of the roots of the quadratic equation.

13. $2x^2 - 13x + 15$ _____

Name: _____ Date: _____

Practice: Quadratic Functions—Parabola Practice Makes Perfect

For this activity, use your own scratch paper to work the problems.

1. Complete the table below:

	Function	Parabola Opens	Narrower or Wider
A.	$f(t) = -3t^2 - 7$		
B.	$g(x) = 7x^2 + 3x$		
C.	$h(x) = 0.56x^2 + 0.4x - 1$		

2. For each quadratic function below, find the vertex for the parabola.

    A. $f(x) = 2x^2 - 7x - 4$ _____

    B. $g(t) = 6t^2 + 3t$ _____

    C. $h(x) = x^2 - 9x + 2$ _____

3. For each quadratic function, find the *x*-intercepts, if they exist.

    A. $f(x) = 2x^2 - 7x - 4$ _____

    B. $g(t) = 6t^2 + 3t$ _____

    C. $h(x) = x^2 - 9x + 2$ _____

4. Using your own graph paper, graph the function given by $f(x) = 2x^2 - 7x - 4$.

Chapter 7: Quadratic Equations and Functions (cont.)

Summary of Quadratic Equations and Functions

Quadratic equations are equations that include a term where the variable is raised to the second power (has an exponent of 2). In addition, no other term can include the variable raised to a higher power. The general form of a quadratic equation is $ax^2 + bx + c = 0$, where a, b, and c can be any real number and $a \neq 0$.

The discriminant of a quadratic equation shows whether or not the equation has rational roots. The formula for the discriminant is $D = b^2 - 4ac$. Remember: If $D = 0$, then the equation has a double root. If $D > 0$, the equation has real roots. If $D < 0$, then the equation has imaginary roots.

- ☐ If $a > 0$, then the parabola opens up, and if $a < 0$, the parabola will open down.
- ☐ If $a > 1$, the parabola will be narrower than the general x^2 parabola.
- ☐ If $0 < a < 1$, the parabola will be wider than the general x^2 parabola.

- ☐ The vertex of the parabola is found at the point $\left(\dfrac{-b}{2a}, f\left(\dfrac{-b}{2a}\right)\right)$.

- ☐ To find the y-intercept: Let $x = 0$, find $f(0)$. Plot the point $(0, f(0))$.
- ☐ To find the x-intercept: Let $y = f(x) = 0$ and solve for x. Use either factoring or the quadratic formula to find x.

Putting all this information together will provide the graph for the given quadratic function.

Tips to Remember

It is easy to tell whether the graph of quadratic function, $f(x) = ax^2 + bx + c$, will be a parabola opening up or opening down. Look at the coefficient a of the ax^2 term of the function rule. If a is positive, the parabola opens up, and if a is negative, the parabola opens down.

When you have determined if the parabola opens up or down, you should have some notion if and where the parabola might cross the x- or y-axis. Finding the vertex lets you know if the parabola has a maximum or minimum value.

Real Life Applications

Quadratic functions are used to describe many phenomena that occur in the world. For example, if a ball is thrown into the air, it follows a parabolic path. The equation that describes the impact of gravity on falling objects is quadratic in form. Perhaps the most visual illustration of a quadratic function in action in the real world is the Gateway Arch in St. Louis, Missouri.

Chapter 8: Variation

Introduction to the Concepts of Variation

When one variable changes in direct relationship to the change of the other, it is called a direct variation. Inverse variation is when one variable varies inversely with the other variable. A joint variation is when a quantity varies directly as the product of two or more other quantities. This section will discuss the different types of variation.

Concepts of Variation

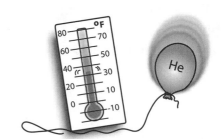

1   Direct Variation and Proportion

2   Inverse and Joint Variation

Explanations of the Concepts of Variation

1   **Direct Variation and Proportion**

Direct variation is when two variable quantities have a constant or unchanged ratio. The constant ratio is the constant of variation. The formula for direct variation is $y = mx$, $(m \neq 0)$. This means that y changes directly as x changes. The constant or the constant of the variation is represented by m.

Example of Direct Variation:

Gina works in a department store earning \$7.50/hour. The constant is m = hourly wage. x = number of hours, and y = amount earned.

$y = \$7.50x \quad (m \neq 0)$

# Hours (x)	Hourly Wage (m) constant of variation	Total Earned (y) $y = mx$
1	\$7.50	$y = \$7.50(1) = \$7.50$
5	\$7.50	$y = \$7.50(5) = \$37.50$
10	\$7.50	$y = \$7.50(10) = \$75.00$
20	\$7.50	$y = \$7.50(20) = \$150.00$
30	\$7.50	$y = \$7.50(30) = \$225.00$
40	\$7.50	$y = \$7.50(40) = \$300.00$

Chapter 8: Variation (cont.)

Using the formula $m = \dfrac{y}{x}$, notice that the variation for each ordered pair is always the same ratio. See the example below.

$$m = \frac{y}{x} = \frac{\$7.50}{1}$$

$$m = \frac{y}{x} = \frac{\$37.50}{5} = \frac{\$7.50}{1}$$

If the ordered pairs are (x_1, y_1) and (x_2, y_2), then $m = \dfrac{y_1}{x_1} \qquad m = \dfrac{y_2}{x_2}$

So $\dfrac{y_1}{x_1} = \dfrac{y_2}{x_2}$

The equality of ratios is called a **proportion**. In direct variation, y is said to be directly proportional to x, and m is the constant of proportionality. A proportion is sometimes written as $y_1 : x_1 = y_2 : x_2$, or y_1 is to x_1 as y_2 is to x_2. The x_1 and y_2 in this statement are called the **means**, and the y_1 and the x_2 are the **extremes**. In any proportion, the product of the extremes equals the product of the means, so $y_1 x_2 = x_1 y_2$.

Example of Product of Extremes and Means:

Problem: If y varies directly as x, and $y = 15$ when $x = 24$, find x when $y = 25$.

$$x_2 = ? \qquad y_2 = 25 \qquad x_1 = 24 \qquad y_1 = 15$$

Step 1: $y_1 x_2 = x_1 y_2$

$x_2(15) = 24(25)$

Step 2: $15x_2 = 600$

Step 3: $\dfrac{15x_2}{15} = \dfrac{600}{15}$

Answer: $x_2 = 40$

Chapter 8: Variation (cont.)

2 Inverse and Joint Variation

Inverse variation is when one variable varies inversely with the other variable. An inverse variation is defined by an equation of the form $xy = k$ or $y = \dfrac{k}{x}$ ($x \neq 0$ and $k \neq 0$). In this case, y varies inversely as x, or y is inversely proportional to x. The constant k is the constant of variation or the constant of proportionality. In inverse variation, as one variable increases, the other decreases. In inverse variation, $x_1 y_1 = x_2 y_2$.

Example of Inverse Variation:

If y is inversely proportional to x, and $y = 6$ when $x = 5$, find x when $y = 12$.

$xy = k$

$y = \dfrac{k}{x}$ $\qquad$ $6 = \dfrac{k}{5}$ $\qquad$ $6(5) = \dfrac{k}{5}(5)$ $\qquad$ $30 = k$

The formula is $y = \dfrac{30}{x}$

$12 = \dfrac{30}{x}$

$12(x) = \dfrac{30}{x}(x)$

$12x = 30$

$\dfrac{12x}{12} = \dfrac{30}{12}$

$x = \dfrac{30}{12} = \dfrac{5}{2}$

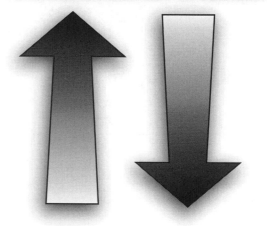

Chapter 8: Variation (cont.)

A **joint variation** is when a quantity varies directly as the product of two or more other quantities. If z varies jointly as x and the square of y, then $z = kxy^2$ ($k \neq 0$).

Example of Joint Variation:

If z varies jointly as x and the square root of y, then $z = k(x)(\sqrt{y})$.

$z = 6$ when $x = 3$ and $y = 16$, find z when $x = 7$ and $y = 4$.

$z = k(x)(\sqrt{y})$

$6 = k(3)(\sqrt{16})$

$6 = k(3)(4)$

$6 = 12k$

$\dfrac{6}{12} = \dfrac{12k}{12}$

$\dfrac{1}{2} = k$

The equation of the joint variation is $z = \frac{1}{2}x\sqrt{y}$

$z = \frac{1}{2}x\sqrt{y}$

$z = \frac{1}{2}(7)\sqrt{4}$

$z = \frac{1}{2}(7)(2)$

$z = \frac{1}{2}(14)$

$z = 7$

Name: _____ Date: _____

Chapter 8: Variation (cont.)

Practice: Variation

Show your work for the following problems.
Direct Variation

1. If *y* varies directly as *x,* and *y* = 15 when *x* = 24, find *x* when *y* = 30.

   x = _____

2. If *y* varies directly as *x,* and *y* = 6 when *x* = 15, find *y* when *x* = 25.

   x = _____

3. If *a* is directly proportional to *b,* and *a* = 9 when *b* = 7.5, find *b* when *a* = 24.

   b = _____

Inverse and Joint Variation

4. If *y* is inversely proportional to *x,* and *y* = 12 when *x* = 5, find *x* when *y* = 18.

   x = _____

5. If *z* is jointly proportional to *x* and *y,* and *z* = 18 when *x* = 0.4 and *y* = 3, find *z* when *x* = 1.2 and *y* = 2.

   z = _____

Chapter 8: Variation (cont.)

Summary of Variation

Direct variation is when two variable quantities have a constant or unchanged ratio. The constant ratio is the constant of variation. The formula for direct variation is $y = mx$, $(m \neq 0)$.

The equality of ratios is called a proportion. In direct variation, y is said to be directly proportional to x, and m is the constant of proportionality. A proportion is sometimes written as $y_1 : x_1 = y_2 : x_2$, or y_1 is to x_1 as y_2 is to x_2. The x_1 and y_2 in this statement are called the means, and the y_1 and the x_2 are the extremes. In any proportion, the product of the extremes equals the product of the means.

An inverse variation is when one variable varies inversely with the other variable. As one variable increases, the other variable decreases.

A joint variation is when a quantity varies directly as the product of two or more other quantities.

Tips to Remember

When working with variation, keep in mind the following:
- ☐ Make sure you know whether the variation is direct, inverse, or joint.
- ☐ For direct variation, remember that the product of the means equals the product of the extremes.
- ☐ For inverse variation, remember that as the value of one variable increases, the value of the other decreases.
- ☐ Use the appropriate arithmetic and algebra rules to solve for the unknown value.
- ☐ Check the values to determine if your solution makes sense.

Real Life Applications of Variation

Direct variation can be used to determine salaries based on an hourly rate. It can also be used to determine the pressure of water at various depths in the ocean.

Answer Keys

Chapter 1: Practice: Solving Equations and Problems (pages 21–22)

Simplifying Expressions

1. $4 \quad (2 + 2) - 1$
    $4 \quad 4 - 1$
    $1 - 1 = 0$

2. $(5 - 3)^2(2 - 1)$
    $(2)^2(1)$
    $(4)(1) = 4$

3. $5x - (6 - 3) + 7$
    $5x - 3 + 7$
    $5x + 4$

Simplify each side of the equation

4. $4a + 5a - 2 = 5 + 3 - 1$
    $9a - 2 = 7$

5. $3x - 2x + x - 4 + 3 - 2 = 0$
    $2x - 3 = 0$

6. $3(x + 5) = 0$
    $3x + 15 = 0$
    This could also
    be simplified.
    $$\frac{3(x + 5)}{3} = \frac{0}{3}$$
    $x + 5 = 0$

7. $3x - 2x = 6 - 9$
    $x = \text{-}3$

8. $3x + 4x = 6(2x + 1)$
    $7x = 12x + 6$

Solving Equations with One Variable

9. $4a + 5a - 2 = 5 + 3 - 1$
    $9a - 2 = 7$
    $9a - 2 + 2 = 7 + 2$
    $9a = 9$
    $$\frac{9a}{9} = \frac{9}{9}$$
    $a = 1$

10. $3x - 2x + x - 4 + 3 - 2 = 0$
    $x = \frac{3}{2}$

11. $3(x + 5) = 0$
    $x = \text{-}5$

12. $3x - 2x = 6 - 9$
    $x = \text{-}3$

13. $3x + 4x = 6(2x + 1)$
    $x = \text{-}\frac{6}{5}$

Words Into Symbols

14. $n^3 - n$ 15. $3(n + 7)$ 16. $A = 2w(w)$ or $A = 2w^2$ 17. $24p = \$1.00$
18. $n = 80 - 13$ 19. $3r + 1(r + 10); \ 3r + 1r + 10; \ 4r + 10$

Write an Equation

20. $n = $ number of boys $(2n - 6) + n = 75$ 21. $r = $ regular price $r + 3(r - 5) = 50$

Problem Solving With Equations

22. $332 = 5000 \quad i \qquad \dfrac{332}{5000} = \dfrac{5000i}{5000} \qquad 0.0664 = i$ This could also be written as 6.64%.

Chapter 2: Practice: Inequalities (pages 33–35)

Inequalities

1. $3 > 7$ False 2. $6 \geq 8$ False   3. $6 \leq 6$ True   4. $0 < \text{-}6$ False   5. $\text{-}6 \leq \text{-}1$ True
6. $a < 5$; a is less than five; Numbers that make the inequality true: Any number less than five
7. $c \geq 2$; c is greater than or equal to two; Numbers that make the inequality true: Any number equal to two or greater than two
8. $x \leq 0$; x is less than or equal to 0; Numbers that make the inequality true: Any number equal to zero or less than zero

Graphing Inequalities

9. $n \leq 10$

116

10. $b \geq -4$

11. $x < -\dfrac{3}{4}$

12. $x > 4$

Solving Inequalities: #13 is worked out completely as an example.

13. $3x > 9$
      Simplify each side of the inequality: Inequality is simplified.
      Use addition and/or subtraction: Nothing to add or subtract.
      Multiplication and/or division:

      $$\dfrac{3x}{3} > \dfrac{9}{3}$$

      $x > 3$
      Check the problem: Pick a number that makes the statement true. 4 > 3 makes the statement true.
      Substitute 4 in the original inequality and see if it makes the statement true.
      $3(4) > 9$ $12 > 9$ This statement is true, so the solution is correct.
      Graphing the Inequality:

      Checking the Inequality Graph: Substitute one of the numbers included for the variable. 4 > 3
      This statement is true.
      Substitute zero for the variable 0 > 3. This is not true, and zero is not included, so the direction of
      the arrow is correct.

14. $\dfrac{1}{2}x \leq 4$ $x \leq 8$

15. $2(y + 1) + 3 < y$ $2y + 5 < y$ $y < -5$

16. $-\dfrac{3}{2}x < -12$ $x > 8$

Conjunctions and Disjunctions: #17 is worked out completely as an example.

17. $3 < 2x + 5$ and $2x + 5 \leq 15$
      Simplify each side of the inequality.
      Use addition and/or subtraction.
      $3 < 2x + 5$ and $2x + 5 \leq 15$
      $3 - 5 < 2x + 5 - 5$ $2x + 5 - 5 \leq 15 - 5$
      $-2 < 2x$ $2x \leq 10$
      Multiplication and/or division
      $\dfrac{-2}{2} < \dfrac{2x}{2}$ $\dfrac{2x}{2} \leq \dfrac{10}{2}$
      $-1 < x$ $x \leq 5$

Check the problems: Pick a number that makes the statements true. -1 < 3 and 3 ≤ 5 makes these statements true. Substitute 3 in both of the original inequalities and see if it makes the statement true. Remember that in conjunctions, both have to be true.

$3 < 2x + 5$ and $2x + 5 ≤ 15$
$3 < 2(3) + 5$ $2(3) + 5 ≤ 15$
$3 < 6 + 5$ $6 + 5 ≤ 15$
$3 < 11$ $11 ≤ 15$

Both statements are true, so the solution was correct.
Graph the Conjunction:

Check the Inequality Graph:
$-1 < x$ and $x ≤ 5$
Substitute one of the numbers included for the variable. -1 < 2 and 2 ≤ 5
-1 < 2 is true and 2 ≤ 5 is true
Substitute zero for the variable -1 < 0 and 0 ≤ 5. Both statements are true, so zero is included.
This is a conjunction because both statements are true.

18. $7 - 2y ≤ 1$ or $3y + 10 < 4 - y$

     $y ≥ 3$ $y < -\frac{3}{2}$ This is a disjunction because one statement is true and one is false.

Match the Graph With the Open Sentences
19.   b   20.   a
Working With Absolute Values

21. $|3t - 1| > 2$ Equivalent Sentences $3t - 1 > 2$ or $3t - 1 < -2$

                                                $t > 1$ or $t < -\frac{1}{3}$

Graph: The solution set is $t > 1$ or $t < -\frac{1}{3}$

Chapter 3: Practice: Linear Equations and Inequalities (pages 48–50)
Solving Linear Equations With Two Variables

1. $3x + 2y = 7$ Solution Set $\{x, y\}$ $\{(0, \frac{7}{2}), (1, 2), (2, \frac{1}{2}), (3, -1), (4, -\frac{5}{2})\}$
2. $y = 8x + 16$ Solution Set $\{x, y\}$ $\{(0, 16), (1, 24), (2, 32), (3, 40), (4, 48)\}$
3. $y = 4x + 20$
     Solution Set $\{x, y\}$
     $\{(0, 20), (1, 24), (2, 28), (3, 32), (4, 36)\}$

Graphing Linear Equations With Two Variables

4. $3x + 2y = 7$
5. $y = 8x + 16$
6. $y = 4x + 20$

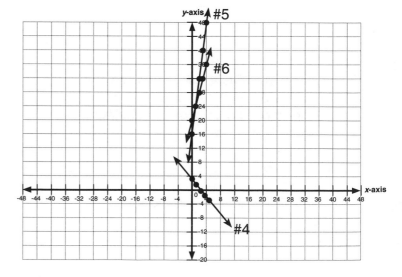

7. Using the graphs in problems 4–6, what would y be if $x = -2$?

   Problem A: $3x + 2y = 7$ If $x = -2$, then $y = \frac{13}{2}$
   Problem B: $y = 8x + 16$ If $x = -2$, then $y = 0$
   Problem C: $y = 4x + 20$ If $x = -2$, then $y = 12$

8. Using the formulas, check your answers in number 7.

   Problem A: $3x + 2y = 7$ **Problem B:** $y = 8x + 16$ **Problem C:** $y = 4x + 20$
   If $x = -2$ If $x = -2$ If $x = -2$
   $3(-2) + 2y = 7$ $y = 8(-2) + 16$ $y = 4(-2) + 20$
   $-6 + 2y = 7$ $y = -16 + 16$ $y = -8 + 20$
   $-6 + 6 + 2y = 7 + 6$ $y = 0$ $y = 12$
   $2y = 13$
   $\frac{2y}{2} = \frac{13}{2}$

   $y = \frac{13}{2}$

Graph the Linear Inequality

9. $3x + 2y + 4 \geq 0$

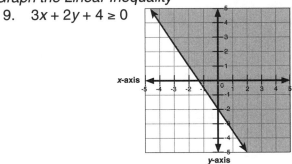

10. $5x - 4y > 10$

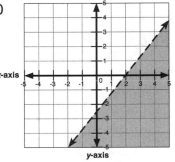

Solving Systems of Equations

11. $x + 4y = 17$ and $-x - 2y = -9$
    Add the equations.

    $\quad x + 4y = 17$
    $\underline{+ (-x - 2y = -9)}$
    $\qquad\quad 2y = 8$

    Solve the resulting equation.
    $\frac{2y}{2} = \frac{8}{2}$

    $y = 4$
    Check the answers:
    $x + 4y = 17$
    $1 + 4(4) = 17$
    $1 + 16 = 17$
    $17 = 17$

    Substitute the answer back into one of the equations to solve for the other variable.
    $x + 4y = 17$
    $x + 4(4) = 17$
    $x + 16 = 17$
    $x + 16 - 16 = 17 - 16$
    $x = 1$

    $-x - 2y = -9$
    $-1 - 2(4) = -9$
    $-1 - 8 = -9$
    $-9 = -9$

12. $\frac{1}{4}x + 3y = 6$ and $\frac{1}{4}x + y = 4$
    $y = 1$ $x = 12$

13. $3x - 2y = 9$ $-x + 3y = 4$
    Multiply the first equation by the coefficient   Multiply the second equation by the coefficient
    in front of the x in the second equation.   in front of the x of the first equation.
    $-1(3x - 2y = 9)$ $3(-x + 3y = 4)$
    $-1(3x) - -1(2y) = -1(9)$ $3(-x) + 3(3y) = 3(4)$
    $-3x + 2y = -9$ $-3x + 9y = 12$

Add or subtract these two new equations. Coefficients are the same, so subtract.

$-3x + 2y = -9$

$- (-3x + 9y = 12)$

$\overline{\qquad -7y = -21}$

Solve the resulting equation.

$\dfrac{-7y}{-7} = \dfrac{-21}{-7}$

$y = 3$

Substitute the answer back into one of the equations to solve for the other variable.

$-x + 3y = 4$

$-x + 3(3) = 4$

$-x + 9 = 4$

$-x + 9 - 9 = 4 - 9$

$-x = -5$

$\dfrac{-1x}{-1} = \dfrac{-5}{-1}$

$x = 5$

14. $x - 3y = 0$ $x + 3y = 6$

      $x = 3$ $y = 1$

Chapter 4: Practice: Polynomial Products and Factors (pages 60–61)

Simplifying Polynomials

1. $2x - 5x^2 + 3 + x^2 - 1 + 2x$

    $-4x^2 + 4x + 2$

2. $4x - 3x^3 + 6 + x^2 + 1x^3 + 1x$

    $-2x^3 + x^2 + 5x + 6$

Adding Polynomials

3. $7x^2 + 2x + 5$ and $3x^3 + 2x^2 + 4x - 1$

    $3x^3 + 2x^2 + 4x - 1$

    $\underline{+ \qquad 7x^2 + 2x + 5}$

    $3x^3 + 9x^2 + 6x + 4$

4. $x^2 + 6x + 5$ and $3x^3 + 2x^2 + 4x - 1$

    $3x^3 + 2x^2 + 4x - 1$

    $\underline{+ \qquad x^2 + 6x + 5}$

    $3x^3 + 3x^2 + 10x + 4$

Subtracting Polynomials

5. $3 + 2x^3 + 2x + 3$ from $3x^3 + 2x^2 + 4x - 1$

     $3x^3 + 2x^2 + 4x - 1$

     $\underline{- (2x^3 + \qquad + 2x - 6)}$

       $x^3 + 2x^2 + 2x + 5$

6. $2x^2 + 6x - 3x^3$ from $3x^3 + 2x^2 + 4x - 1$

     $3x^3 + \; 2x^2 + 4x - 1$

     $\underline{- (-3x^3 + \; 2x^2 + 6x)}$

      $6x^3 + \; 0 - \; 2x - 1$ Simplified: $6x^3 - 2x - 1$

Laws of Exponents

7. $3a^3 \bullet 4a^4 = 12a^{3+4} = 12a^7$ (Law 1)

8. $(2c^2 d^3)^3 = 2^3 c^6 d^9 = 8c^6 d^9$ (Law 3)

9. $(xy)^3 = x^3 y^3$ (Law 2)

10. $3x^2 \bullet 2x^4 = 6x^{2+4} = 6x^6$ (Law 1)

11. $(4b^2 c)^3 = (4)^3 b^{2 \bullet 3} c^{1 \bullet 3} = 64b^6 c^3$ (Law 3)

12. $(yz)^5 = y^5 z^5$ (Law 2)

Multiplying Polynomials

13. $(3x + 1)(2x - 7)$

     Multiply each term of one by each term of the other.

     $3x(2x - 7) + 1(2x - 7)$

     $6x^2 - 21x + 2x - 7$

     Add them together.

       $6x^2 - 21x$

     $\underline{+ \qquad\quad 2x - 7}$

      $6x^2 - 19x - 7$

14. $(5a - 9)(3a + 2) = 15a^2 - 17a - 18$

15. $(2y - 3)^2 = 4y^2 - 12y + 9$

16. $(x^2 + 2x + 3)(2x^2 - 2x + 2)$

     $= 2x^4 + 2x^3 + 4x^2 - 2x + 6$

Factoring Polynomials

17. $a^2 + 6a + 9$ Perfect Square Trinomial

     $(a + 3)^2$

18. $25x^2 - 16a^2$

     $(5x + 4a)(5x - 4a)$

19. $8x^3 + y^3$
$(2x)^3 + y^3$
$(2x + y)(4x^2 - 2xy + y^2)$

20. $9x^2 - 12x + 4$
$(3x - 2)^2$
Perfect Square Trinomial

Solving Polynomial Equations

21. $y^2 = y + 12$
Write the equation = to 0.
$y^2 - y - 12 = y + 12 - y - 12$
$y^2 - y - 12 = 0$
Factor the other side.
$(y + 3)(y - 4) = 0$
Write each factor as an equation that is equal to 0.
$y + 3 = 0$ $\qquad$ $y - 4 = 0$
Solve the equations.
$y + 3 - 3 = 0 - 3$ $\qquad$ $y - 4 + 4 = 0 + 4$
$y = -3$ $\qquad$ $y = 4$ $\qquad$ The solution set is {-3, 4}.

22. $x^2 = x + 30$ $\qquad$ Solution set is {-5, 6}.

Problem Solving Using Polynomial Equations

23. Speed = v = 96 ft./sec. $\qquad$ Time = ? $\qquad$ Height = ?
Write the equation = to 0.
$h = vt - 16t^2$
Height when it starts and finishes is 0. $\qquad$ $vt - 16t^2 = 0$
Velocity is 96 ft./sec., so $v = 96t$. $\qquad$ $96t - 16t^2 = 0$
Factor the other side.
$16t$ is the GCF.
$16t(6 - t)$
Write each factor as an equation that is equal to 0.
$16t = 0$ $\qquad$ $6 - t = 0$
Solve the equations.
$16t = 0$ $\qquad$ $6 - t = 0$
$\dfrac{16t}{16} = \dfrac{0}{16}$ $\qquad$ $6 - t + t = 0 + t$
$\qquad\qquad\qquad$ $6 = t$
$t = 0$
The rocket went up, so the answer cannot be 0. The rocket is in the air 6 seconds.

Chapter 5: Practice: Rational Expressions (pages 73–74)

Laws of Exponents

1. $\dfrac{3^7}{3^4} = 3^{7-4} = 3^3 = 27$
2. $\dfrac{3x^2}{x^6} = \dfrac{3}{x^4}$
3. $\left(\dfrac{t^2}{3}\right)^3 = \dfrac{t^{2 \cdot 3}}{3^3} = \dfrac{t^6}{27}$
4. $\dfrac{24x^3}{4x} = 6x^2$

Using Scientific Notation

5. $0.000000789 = 7.89 \quad 10^{-7}$
6. $186,000 = 1.86 \quad 10^5$
7. $6.75 \quad 10^4 = 67,500$
8. $7.50 \quad 10^{-10} = 0.000000000750$

Multiplying and Dividing Rational Expressions

9. $\dfrac{5x^3}{-3} \cdot \dfrac{-6}{10x^2}$

Divide by common factors x^2, -3, 5

$\dfrac{x}{1} \cdot \dfrac{2}{2} = x$

10. $\dfrac{x^2}{4} \cdot \left(\dfrac{xy}{6}\right)^{-1} \cdot \dfrac{2y^2}{x} = \dfrac{3y}{1} = 3y$

11. $\dfrac{8a^2}{3} \div \dfrac{2a}{9} = \dfrac{4a}{1} \cdot \dfrac{3}{1} = 12a$

12. $\dfrac{x^2-4}{2x^2-5x+2} \div \dfrac{2x^2-3x-2}{4x^2-1} = \dfrac{x+2}{x-2}$

Adding and Subtracting Rational Expressions

13. $\dfrac{3}{15} - \dfrac{10}{15} + \dfrac{5}{15} = \dfrac{-2}{15}$

14. $\dfrac{x+2}{12} + \dfrac{x-2}{6} = \dfrac{x+2x+2-4}{12} = \dfrac{3x-2}{12}$

15. $\dfrac{1}{x^2-1} - \dfrac{1}{(x-1)^2} = \dfrac{x-1-x-1}{(x-1)(x+1)(x-1)} = \dfrac{-2}{(x+1)(x-1)^2}$

16. $\dfrac{3}{a^2-5a+6} + \dfrac{2}{a^2-4} = \dfrac{5a}{(a-2)(a-3)(a+2)}$

Solving Fractional Equations and Inequalities

17. $\dfrac{x^2}{3} - \dfrac{x}{6} = 1$ LCD is 6. Multiply both sides by the LCD 6. $6(\dfrac{x^2}{3} - \dfrac{x}{6}) = 1(6)$

Reduce the fractions. $2x^2 - x = 6$
Solve the equation by making it = 0.
$2x^2 - x - 6 = 6 - 6$
$2x^2 - x - 6 = 0$
Factor the left side.
$(2x+3)(x-2) = 0$
Set each factor = 0

$2x + 3 = 0$ 　　　　$x - 2 = 0$
$2x + 3 - 3 = 0 - 3$ 　$x - 2 + 2 = 0 + 2$
$2x = -3$ 　　　　　$x = 2$
$\dfrac{2x}{2} = \dfrac{-3}{2}$

$x = -\dfrac{3}{2}$ 　　Solution set is {x: 2, $-\dfrac{3}{2}$}

18. $\dfrac{x(x+1)}{5} - \dfrac{x+1}{6} = \dfrac{1}{3}$

Solution set is {$-\dfrac{5}{3}$, $\dfrac{3}{2}$}

19. $\dfrac{y^2+4}{6} + \dfrac{y+1}{3} < \dfrac{3}{2}$

Solution: $y < 1$ 　$y > -3$

20. What was the length of the side of the original square?

Let x represent the side of the square. Fred did $\dfrac{(x-1)^2}{3}$. Here is what Frank did $\dfrac{x+2}{2}$.

Fred's answer = Frank's answer, so we know that the two expressions are equal.

$\dfrac{(x-1)^2}{3} = \dfrac{x+2}{2}$

$3(\dfrac{(x-1)^2}{3}) = 3(\dfrac{x+2}{2})$

$2(x^2 - 2x + 1) = 2(\dfrac{3x+6}{2})$

$2x^2 - 4x + 2 = 3x + 6$
$2x^2 - 4x - 3x + 2 = 3x + 6 - 3x$
$2x^2 - 7x + 2 - 6 = 6 - 6$
$2x^2 - 7x - 4 = 0$
Factor.
$(2x+1)(x-4) = 0$

Set each one = 0 and solve for x.   Check the solutions.

$2x + 1 = 0$ $x - 4 = 0$ $2x^2 - 7x - 4 = 0$ $2x^2 - 7x - 4 = 0$

$2x + 1 - 1 = 0 - 1$ $x - 4 + 4 = 0 + 4$ $2(-\frac{1}{2})^2 - 7(-\frac{1}{2}) - 4 = 0$ $2(4)^2 - 7(4) - 4 = 0$

$2x = -1$ $x = 4$ $2(\frac{1}{4}) + 3\frac{1}{2} - 4 = 0$ $2(16) - 28 - 4 = 0$

$\dfrac{2x}{2} = \dfrac{-1}{2}$ $\frac{1}{2} + 3\frac{1}{2} - 4 = 0$ $32 - 32 = 0$

                                         $4 - 4 = 0$ $0 = 0$

$x = -\frac{1}{2}$ $0 = 0$

Length of side must equal 4, since it cannot be a negative number.

Chapter 6: Practice: Roots, Radicals, and Complex Numbers (pages 91–92)

Roots and Radicals

1. $\sqrt{\dfrac{1}{64}} = \dfrac{1}{8}$

2. $\sqrt[3]{a^6} = a^2$ Divide the index (3) into the power of a (6).

3. $\sqrt{13^6} = 13^3 = 2{,}197$
   Divide the implied index (2) into the power of 6.

Products and Quotients

4. $\sqrt{\dfrac{50}{49}} = \dfrac{5\sqrt{2}}{7}$

5. $\sqrt[3]{\dfrac{2}{9}} = \dfrac{\sqrt[3]{6}}{3}$

6. $\sqrt{6} \cdot \sqrt{\dfrac{2}{3}} = 2$

7. $\sqrt[3]{\dfrac{27a}{4b^4}} = \dfrac{3\sqrt[3]{2ab^2}}{2b^2}$

Sums of Radicals

8. $\sqrt{50} + \sqrt{18} = 8\sqrt{2}$

9. $\sqrt{6} + \sqrt{36} + \sqrt{216} = 6 + 7\sqrt{6}$

10. $\sqrt{\dfrac{27}{5}} - \sqrt{\dfrac{3}{5}} = \dfrac{2\sqrt{15}}{5}$

11. $\dfrac{\sqrt[3]{18} + 3\sqrt[3]{54}}{\sqrt[3]{3}} = \sqrt[3]{6} + 3\sqrt[3]{18}$

Simplify Binomials With Radicals

12. $(2\sqrt{3} - \sqrt{6})^2$ Remember $(a - b)^2 = a^2 - 2ab + b^2$
    $(2\sqrt{3})^2 - 2 \cdot 2\sqrt{3} \cdot \sqrt{6} + (\sqrt{6})^2 = 18 - 12\sqrt{2}$

13. $(4\sqrt{5} + 3\sqrt{2})(4\sqrt{5} - 3\sqrt{2}) = (4\sqrt{5})^2 - (3\sqrt{2})^2 = 62$

14. $\dfrac{3 + \sqrt{5}}{3 - \sqrt{5}} = \dfrac{7 + 3\sqrt{5}}{2}$

Solving Equations With Radicals

15. $3x - 5\sqrt{x} = 2$
    Isolate the radical. $3x - 5\sqrt{x} + 5\sqrt{x} = 2 + 5\sqrt{x} - 2$
    $3x - 2 = 5\sqrt{x}$
    Square both sides. $(3x - 2)^2 = (5\sqrt{x})^2$
    $9x^2 - 12x + 4 = 25x$
    Solve the equation.
    $9x^2 - 12x + 4 - 25x = 25x - 25x$
    $9x^2 - 37x + 4 = 0$
    $(x - 4)(9x - 1) = 0$

Check the solutions.

$x - 4 = 0$ $9x - 1 = 0$ $3(4) - 5\sqrt{4} = 2$ $3(\frac{1}{9}) - 5\sqrt{\frac{1}{9}} \neq 2$

$x - 4 + 4 = 0 + 4$ $9x - 1 + 1 = 0 + 1$ $12 - 5(2) = 2$ $\frac{1}{3} - 5(\frac{1}{3}) \neq 2$

$x = 4$ $9x = 1$ $12 - 10 = 2$ $\frac{1}{3} - \frac{5}{3} \neq 2$

                     $\dfrac{9x}{9} = \dfrac{1}{9}$ $x = \frac{1}{9}$ $2 = 2$ $\frac{4}{3} \neq 2$

                                        The solution is 4.   This shows an extraneous solution.

16. $2\sqrt[3]{x} = \sqrt[3]{x^2}$ Solution set is {8, 0}.

Radical Equations and Linear Radical Equations

17. $5\sqrt{x} = 10$
Radical Equation: Square both sides.
$(5\sqrt{x})^2 = 10^2$
$25x = 100$
$\dfrac{25x}{25} = \dfrac{100}{25}$
$x = 4$

18. $x\sqrt{5} = 10$
Linear Equation: Solve without squaring both sides.
$\dfrac{x\sqrt{5}}{\sqrt{5}} = \dfrac{10}{\sqrt{5}}$

$x = \dfrac{10}{\sqrt{5}}$ $x = \dfrac{10}{\sqrt{5}} \cdot \dfrac{\sqrt{5}}{\sqrt{5}}$

$x = \dfrac{10\sqrt{5}}{5}$ $x = 2\sqrt{5}$

Decimal Representation

19. $\dfrac{5}{8} = 0.625$ 20. $\dfrac{13}{7} = 1.\overline{857142}$ 21. $\dfrac{13}{4} = 3.25$

Complex Numbers

22. $(3 + 6i) - (4 - 2i)$
$(3 - 4) + (6 + 2)i$
$-1 + 8i$

23. $(3 + 4i)^2$
$-7 + 24i$

24. $\dfrac{2}{3 - i} = \dfrac{3}{5} + \dfrac{i}{5}$

Chapter 7: Practice: Quadratic Equations (page 107)

Forming a Quadratic Equation From a Linear Equation By the Variable in the Equation

1. $x(5x + 8) = 0$ $5x^2 + 8x = 0$ 2. $-a(10a - 2) = 0$ $-10a^2 + 2a = 0$
3. $4x(2x - 3) = -3$ $8x^2 - 12x = -3$ or $8x^2 - 12x + 3 = 0$

Forming Quadratic Equations By Multiplying Binomial Expressions

4. $(2c - 5)(3c + 1) = 0$ $6c^2 + 2c - 15c - 5 = 0$ $6c^2 - 13c - 5 = 0$
5. $(x + 2)(x - 3) = 0$ $x^2 - 3x + 2x - 6 = 0$ $x^2 - x - 6 = 0$

Use Factoring to Solve

6. $3x^2 - 27 = 0$ $x = 3$ or -3 7. $2a^2 - 6a = 0$ $a = 0$ or 3

8. $2b^2 + 7b = -6$ $b = -2$ or $-\dfrac{3}{2}$

Use the Complete the Square Method to Solve

9. $x^2 + 6x + 7 = 0$ $x = -3 + \sqrt{2}$ or $x = -3 - \sqrt{2}$

Use the Quadratic Formula to Solve

10. $2x^2 + 5x + 2 = 0$ $x = -2$ or $-\dfrac{1}{2}$ 11. $3x^2 + x - 2 = 0$ $x = -1$ or $\dfrac{2}{3}$

Solve Using a Quadratic Equation

12. The dimensions are 4 meters by 12 meters or 6 meters by 8 meters.

Roots of Quadratic Equations: Without solving, determine the nature of the roots.

13. $2x^2 - 13x + 15$ $D = (-13)2 - 4(2)(15)$ $D = 169 - 120 = 49$
This equation has integral coefficients, and the answer is positive and a perfect square, so the roots are real, unequal, and rational.

Chapter 7: Practice: Quadratic Functions—Parabola Practice Makes Perfect (page 108)

1.

	Function	Parabola Opens	Narrower or Wider
A.	$f(t) = -3t^2 - 7$	Down	Narrower
B.	$g(x) = 7x^2 + 3x$	Up	Narrower
C.	$h(x) = 0.56x^2 + 0.4x - 1$	Up	Wider

2. For each quadratic function below, find the vertex for the parabola.

   A. $f(x) = 2x^2 - 7x - 4$ VERTEX: $(\frac{7}{4}, -\frac{81}{8})$ or (1.75, -10.125)

   B. $g(t) = 6t^2 + 3t$ VERTEX: $(-\frac{1}{4}, -\frac{3}{8})$ or (-0.25, -0.375)

   C. $h(x) = x^2 - 9x + 2$ VERTEX: $(\frac{9}{2}, -\frac{73}{4})$ or (4.5, -18.25)

3. For each quadratic function, find the x-intercepts, if they exist.

   A. $f(x) = 2x^2 - 7x - 4$

   Use factoring: $x = -\frac{1}{2}$ $x = 4$ So, $(-\frac{1}{2}, 0)$ and (4, 0) are the x-intercepts for the parabola.

   B. $g(t) = 6t^2 + 3t$

   Use factoring: $t = 0$ $t = -\frac{1}{2}$ So, (0, 0) and $(-\frac{1}{2}, 0)$ are the x-intercepts for the parabola.

   C. $h(x) = x^2 - 9x + 2$

   Use the Quadratic Formula: $x \approx 8.77$ $x \approx 0.23$ So, (8.77, 0) and (0.23, 0) are the x-intercepts for the parabola, rounded to two decimal places.

4. Graph function given by $f(x) = 2x^2 - 7x - 4$.
   Use the information in Problems #1, #2, and #3.
   Should have a parabola that opens up and is narrower than the x^2 parabola.

   VERTEX: $(\frac{7}{4}, -\frac{81}{8})$ or (1.75, -10.125)

   x-intercepts: $(-\frac{1}{2}, 0)$ and (4, 0)
   In addition, the point (0, -4) is on the graph.
   It is the y-intercept of the parabola.

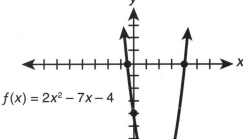

$f(x) = 2x^2 - 7x - 4$

Chapter 8: Practice: Variation (page114–115)

Direct Variation

1. If y varies directly as x, and $y = 15$ when $x = 24$, find x when $y = 30$.

   $y = mx$

   $15 = m(24)$ The equation of the direct variation is $y = \frac{5}{8}x$.

   $\frac{15}{24} = \frac{24m}{24}$ $y = \frac{5}{8}x$

                                  $30 = \frac{5}{8}x$

   $\frac{15}{24} = m$ $30(\frac{8}{5}) = \frac{5}{8}x(\frac{8}{5})$

   $\frac{5}{8} = m$ $48 = x$

2. $m = \frac{2}{5}$ $y = 10$ 3. $a_1b_2 = a_1b_2$ $b_2 = 20$

Inverse and Joint Variation

4. $k = 90$ $x = \frac{15}{2}$ 5. $k = 15$ $z = 36$

125

References

Brown, R., Dolciani, M., Sorgenfrey, R., Cole, W., (1997). *Algebra structure and method book 1.* Evanston, IL: McDougal Littell.

Chicago Mathematics Project. *Connected mathematics.* University of Chicago. Found online at: http://www.math.msu.edu/cmp/curriculum/Algebra.htm

Edwards, E. (1990). *Algebra for everyone.* Reston, VA: National Council of Teachers of Mathematics.

Long, L. (1998). *Painless algebra.* Hauppauge, NY: Barron's Educational Series.

National Council for Teachers of Mathematics. (2000). *Principles and standards for school mathematics.* Reston, VA: National Council of Teachers of Mathematics.

National Council of Teachers of Mathematics (NCTM). (2004). *Standards and expectations for algebra.* Reston, VA: National Council of Teachers of Mathematics. Found online at: http://www.nctm.org

Freudenthal Institute at the University of Utrecht/University of Wisconsin/NSF. *Math in context.* Found online at http://showmecenter.missouri.edu/showme/mic.shtml Encyclopedia Britannica.

Web Resources

Reichman, H. and Kohn, M. (2004). *Math made easy.* Found Online at: http://www.mathmadeeasy.com/algebra.html

Algebra.help. (2001–2004). *Algebra help.* Found online at: http://www.algebrahelp.com/index.jsp

Algebra Solutions
http://www.gomath.com/algebra.html

Brennon, J. (2002). *Understanding algebra.* Found online at: http://www.jamesbrennan.org/algebra/

Classzone Algebra 1
http://www.classzone.com/books/algebra_1/index.cfm

Math Archives: Topics in Mathematics Algebra
http://www.archives.math.utk.edu/topics/algebra.html

Math for Morons Like Us
http://library.thinkquest.org/20991/alg2/

Reliable problem solving in all subjects that use mathematics for problem solving. Algebra, Physics, Chemistry … from grade school to grad school and beyond.
http://www2.hawaii.edu/suremath/intro_algebra.html

The Math Forum Drexel University (1994–2004). *K–12 Internet Algebra Resources.* Philadelphia, PA: Found online at: http://mathforum.org/algebra/k12.algebra.html

Borenson, H. (2001–2004). *Hands on Equations.* Allentown, PA: Borenson and Associates. Found online at: http://www.borenson.com

Oracle Education Foundation Think Quest Library (2004). *Algebra.* Found online at: http://library.thinkquest.org/10030/algecon.htm

Oswego Public Schools
http://regentsprep.org/Regents/math/variation/Ldirect.htm

Oswego Public Schools Teacher Resource Page—Direct Variation
http://regentsprep.org/Regents/math/variation/Tdirect.htm

University of Akron Theoretical and Applied Mathematics
http://www.math.uakron.edu/~dpstory/mpt_home.html

Ed Helper.com
http://www.edhelper.com/algebra.htm

Introduction to Algebra
http://www.mathleague.com/help/algebra/algebra.htm

History of Algebra
http://www.ucs.louisiana.edu/~sxw8045/history.htm

Surfing the Net With Kids
http://www.surfnetkids.com/algebra.htm

Moses, B. *The algebra project.* Cambridge, MA: The Algebra Project, Inc. Found online at: http://algebra.org/index.html

Interactive Mathematic Miscellany and Puzzles
http://www.cut-the-knot.org/algebra.shtml

Awesome Library—Algebra
http://www.awesomelibrary.org/Classroom/Mathematics/Middle-High_School_Math/Algebra.html

Cool Math Sites
http://www.cte.jhu.edu/techacademy/web/2000/heal/mathsites.htm

SOS Mathematics
http://www.sosmath.com/

Real Life Applications of Math

Applied Academics: Applications of Mathematics—Careers
http://www.bced.gov.bc.ca/careers/aa/lessons/math.htm

Exactly How Is Math Used in Technology?
http://www.math.bcit.ca/examples/index.shtml

Mathematics Association of America—Careers
http://www.maa.org/careers/index.html

NASA Space Link
http://spacelink.msfc.nasa.gov/index.html